In memory of the Opening Ceremony

of the new premises of Yamanouchi Pharma Sp. z o.o.

Warszawa, April 23, 1999

In memory of the Opening Ceremony

of the new premises of Yamanouchi Pharma Sp. z o.o.

Warszawa, April 23, 1999

POLAND

Wojciech Giełżyński
Irena and Jerzy Kostrowicki

Carpathians and Subcarpathians
Polish Uplands
Sudeten and the Silesian Lowland
Wielkopolska Lowland
Mazovia and Podlasie Lowland
Lakeland and Pomerania

Arkady

POLAND

ISBN 83-213-3895-X

Introduction

Before the Polish state was formed and the Poles learned to write, foreigners described it as the "land of Mieszko".

Ibrahim-Ibn-Jacob from Tortosa in Spain left a detailed account of his visit in 965, a year before Poland was christened and became part of European civilization. Although he never reached the "land of Mieszko", he heard a lot about it at the court of Otto I. He wrote that the state was the biggest of all the Slavic countries and it abounded in food, meat and honey. It was located "at the borders of the West". Ibrahim-Ibn-Jacob also stressed the military power of Mieszko who had a detachment of three thousand armed men. This constituted real power at the time. Ibrahim-Ibn-Jacob was acquainted with Poland better than most Western journalists and politicians today who stubbornly claim that Poland is a country somewhere far to the east, or perhaps to the north...

For the Russians, Poland is truly part of the West, while Poles seem to be papists, faithful disciples of the Pope in Rome. Besides, they use the Latin alphabet! They cannot be real Slavs who should be faithful to the Orthodox Church and use a writing originating from the Old-Slavic Cyrillic alphabet.

The Poles may be East for the West and West for the East, but they themselves claim that they live in the very middle of Europe. Geography proves it. The distance from Poland to Portugal is equal to that from Poland to the Ural mountains which mark the border between Europe and Asia. The same is with the distance to the Peloponnesus in Greece and to Nord Cap in Norway.

Since the borders of the Polish state were easily accessible from the east and west, Poland experienced numerous victories and defeats during its history lasting over one thousand years. Its borders extended and shrank, its territory increased and decreased, it moved on the map, and even disappeared from it for a moment!

During the first centuries of its existence, in the reign of the Piasts, Poland was effective in curbing German expansion as well as in conquering new territories both in the east and south (on the other side of the Carpathian mountains). The kingdom was divided into several independent principalities at the beginning of the 12th century. A similar fate met other European states during the feudal epoch. After reunification at the beginning of the 14th century, Poland was much smaller: it had lost Silesia to the Czechs, the territory on the Oder river to Brandenburg (later Prussia,) and the land in the lower reaches of the Vistula river to the Teutonic Order. A certain compensation for these losses were the conquests of the last of the Piast dynasty, Casimir the Great, in the east. He annexed the Halicki Land with Lvov. Cracow was the capital of Poland at that time. Warsaw was still unimportant among Polish cities.

At the turn of the 14th and 15th centuries, a personal union was effected between Poland and Lithuania, a huge pagan country. Thanks to the marriage of Władysław Jagiełło with the Polish Queen Jadwiga, Poland and Lithuania suddenly became the biggest country in Europe and in 1410 it defeated the Teutonic Order at Grunwald, crushing the Order's strength once and for all. Grunwald was one of the biggest battles in the Middle Ages and in consequence of it Poland returned to the Baltic shore half a century later. The kingdom of the Jagiellons included all of Lithuania and White Russia, a big part of the present Ukraine and Latvia, and even part of Rumania for some time!

A counteroffensive started in the 17th century: the Turks from the south, Muscovites from the east, and the Swedes, who used to be very aggressive, from the north. Poland suffered from the "Swedish deluge". The enemy was defeated in effect, but Poland lost some of its territories and never regained its status of a power. Weakened, it was plunged in confusion. In the 18th century its borders were unprotected and foreign armies marched across it freely. Men of intellect tried to introduce reforms to strengthen the Polish administration, economy, culture and armed forces during the period of the Enlightenment. This was achieved with the adoption of the May 3rd Constitution, the second constitution in the world

– after the American one and before the French one. But it came too late! Three neighboring powers: Russia, Prussia, and Austria, effected the final partition of Poland. The Poles cherished hopes once again in the Napoleonic era, believing in Napoleon, the "rainbow of the Franks". The defeat of the Emperor marked the end of Polish independence. But not the end of dreams about regaining it! During the 19th century, the Poles organized several armed uprisings. Without success. And sometimes deceived by promises of help from the West were never kept.

Fate was more favorable to Poland at the end of the First World War. Russia, which governed most of the Polish territories at the time, was the first to be defeated; the other central powers, Germany and the Habsburg dynasty, were next. Even in the wildest dreams the Poles had not expected this! In 1918, Poland regained its independence. Two years later it managed to defend itself against a Bolshevik attack, gaining a spectacular victory in the battle near Warsaw.

The Poles' joy lasted only two decades. They took advantage of their good fortune unifying the territories of the former three partitions. Nevertheless, the country remained weak. On September 1, 1939, Poland was the first to stand up to Hitler but failed to resist the German forces, especially when Stalin treacherously attacked it on September 17. Another partition took place and Poland disappeared from the map again. Over six million people were killed. In spite of it, the spirit of the Polish underground movement was never broken. Polish soldiers continued fighting alongside their Western counterparts at Narvik in Norway, in the French fields and at Tobruk in Libya. Polish pilots played an important role in the Battle of Britain, and the Polish infantry became famous for its victory at Monte Cassino in Italy, which opened the way to Rome. In the last phase of the war, Polish armored brigades participated in the liberation of France and Holland. A strong Polish army was also formed in the USSR; it fought alongside the Red Army to liberate Poland and defeat the Nazi occupants.

Unfortunately, Poles were not fated to partake of the fruits of victory. Treaties signed in Yalta and Potsdam practically gave Poland away under the rule of the USSR. However, the Poles never accepted the communist system and never agreed to the loss of independence. Demonstrations and strikes were staged intermittently against the communist regime: in 1956, 1968, 1970, 1976, and in 1980 when the Solidarity movement activated ten million people. The spirit of the Poles was significantly supported by Karol Wojtyła better known as John Paul II, the Pope from Poland.

Martial Law was introduced on December 13, 1981; Solidarity was suspended. Eight years later, after another wave of strikes, the union was revived; "Round Table" talks with the communists resulted in a political compromise and partly free elections in 1989 which brought a great victory for democracy and accelerated the disintegration of the communist system in the world.

This is already history. Difficult years followed, marked by a reconstruction of the political, social and economic system. The Poles have managed to build a democracy and political pluralism, as well as a market economy, but Solidarity is no longer as important as before. Poland, an object of interest of the whole world for many years, has ceased to inspire political emotions. It can be said that it has become "normal". This has become one of the many countries in Europe facing the difficulties of reconstruction, recession and unemployment. It does not mean, however, that it ceased to be interesting to foreigners. Tourists, who come in growing numbers from the West, do not complain about a lack of attractions.

Those who like comfort can stay in new, luxurious hotels and eat at excellent restaurants. Those who are looking for cultural experiences, will not be disappointed: Polish theater and music hold one of the leading places in the world. Those who are interested in architecture have many interesting monuments to see. Art galleries are also attractive to connoisseurs, although they can hardly compete with France, Italy or Spain, many of the masterpieces having been destroyed in various wars. Amateurs of the folklore can enjoy it in some village enclaves.

Lovers of nature will not be disappointed. There are many beautiful landscapes and unexpected experiences awaiting the visitor. They will be presented in greater detail in the description of the different regions in Poland.

A little encouragement if you please... Do you love the mountains? There are mountains in Poland, not as high as the Alps, but very beautiful. Do you like water routes? Only Finland (but it is much colder there!) can be compared to the Polish lakelands. Do you prefer the sea? Hundreds of kilometers of sandy beaches, the blue of the Baltic sea... And perhaps you are fascinated with old woods and virgin forests? You can even see the king of the woods, the auroch, comparable with the American buffalo.

Travelling? Not bad. Prices? As everywhere... Entertainment? Full choice.

Of one thing you can be sure – wherever you go you will meet with the famous Polish hospitality.

Carpathians and Subcarpathians

The highest peak in Poland, Rysy, is 2 500 meters minus ten centimeters... In comparison with the Himalayas or the Alps, the Polish Tatra are miniature mountains. But they have the same dangerous beauty of craggy peaks, fantastic precipices and abysses.

The Tatra are part of the Carpathian chain, its middle part to be specific. These young mountains are Cretaceous and Tertiary in date, constitute an extension of the Alps; they run in a deep arc from the Danube near the Slovak capital of Bratislava to the Danube at the Iron Gate on the border of Rumania and Serbia.

Since the very beginning of Polish history, the Carpathians have constituted the southern frontier changing only slightly over the centuries. In this mountain chain, only the Tatra, most of which belong to Slovakia, have an alpine character. The Tatra in their higher, eastern part are built mainly of granites, beautifully carved by the glacier which has also left picturesque lakes in the mountains, like the most famous one, the Morskie Oko. The Western Tatra, a bit lower, are built of crystalline schists and limestone and are more rounded in shape. Underground streams and waterfalls and wonderful caves are very exciting for speleologists.

On the steep slopes of the Tatra one can observe the agile chamois (*Rupicapra rupicapra.*) numerous marmots (*Marmota marmota*) high up in the mountain pastures, standing still when they notice approaching tourists and warning the group of danger with a loud whistle. Sometimes bears approach the villages to look through the trash. Wonderful eagles fly over the rocky peaks (but unfortunately, their number is decreasing year by year).

In the mid-19th century, the Tatra mountains were discovered by tourists and poets. Before that time, life went on in complete isolation. The mountaineers living in the Tatra preserved their customs and wore original clothes similar to those of the Balkan peninsula. They lived working in the forests and breeding sheep. Today mountaineers live off tourists... and trips to find work in America. During holidays, they dress up in tight white trousers made of raw linen, embroidered sleeveless jackets or sheepskin coats also without sleeves and wide, stiff hats with round brims adorned with shells. Podhale, a valley at the foot of the Tatra mountains, is the most faithful to traditional clothes, dances and customs.

Tourists, and especially skiers, like the Tatra mountains and Zakopane located there. No other place in Poland is as popular for its fascinating landscapes and slopes. The influx of millions of guests, both in summer and in winter has unfortunately caused Zakopane to lose its character of a big mountain village with unique wooden architecture. Only some specially protected streets have preserved their original appearance. Nature is well protected thanks to the care of the Tatra National Park. It is true that there are almost no natural backwoods, but spruce forests have remained quite healthy. Some mountain pastures (meadows up in the mountains) are especially beautiful in spring when blooming crocuses make them violet. The mountain streams in upper parts of the Tatra are still crystal clear.

The deep Podhale valley located to the north of the Tatra mountains, is crossed by a chain of limestone rocks which form the low picturesque massif of the Pieniny to the east (the highest peak Trzy Korony is 983 m high). Dunajec, the most beautiful mountain river in Poland, crosses it in a deep canyon. Tourists navigate it in rafts steered by mountaineers. The Pieniny massif is part of the National Park. Numerous endemites, plants and animals which do not live anywhere else, have survived there.

Both in Podhale and Pieniny, as well as in the neighboring Spis, peoples living in the Carpathian mountains: Poles, Ruthenians, Wallachians, Slavs, Hungarians, Gypsies and even German settlers, exercised a significant influence upon the culture in this region. This is to be seen in the architecture and decoration of wooden churches and cottages, in dynamic dances requiring the dancers to have acrobatic capabilities (the famous highland robbers folk dance *zbójnicki*, foremost) and the arts. Folk artists make characteristic wooden sculptures and paintings on glass with the ever present motif of the legendary highland robber Janosik who stole from the rich to give to the poor, just like Robin Hood. Numerous folk stories and songs are based on legends about Janosik.

The Beskidy massif is larger, but lower than the Tatra mountains. They have their own lovers among skiers (the best mountains to practice this sport are near Szczyrk and Żywiec), as well as lovers of walks and folklore, which has been preserved in some villages in Beskid Śląski (Silesian Beskid) and Beskid Niski (Low Beskid), inhabited by the Lemk, one of the ethnic groups of Ruthenians. Lemk villages reach as far as Krynica, which became famous in the 19th century as a health resort thanks to the specific climate and the richness of mineral waters. Similar advantages are also encountered in Rabka, a dreamland for children, as well as Szczawnica, Rymanów and Iwonicz.

Wonderful Bieszczady, sandwiched between Slovakia and Ukraine are the easternmost massif of the Carpathian mountains in Poland. Although they are becoming more and more popular, tourists with backpacks can still walk through beautiful forests and mountain pastures covered with high grass and not meet many people. It is easier to encounter a stag or roe deer, or even a wolf or lynx, the biggest predatory cat living in Europe. Sometimes beers are seen as well. One has to keep an eye out for a poisonous viper or a harmless Aesculapian snake which is not to be found almost anywhere outside the Bieszczady.

An artificial reservoir in Solina on the San river, a real paradise for sailors, is an attraction of southeastern Poland. San is a beautiful and relatively clean river. Przemyśl, located on it, has been an important commercial center on the route from Central Europe to the Black Sea since as far back as the 10th century. Several thousand Greek-Catholic and Orthodox believers live here. Podkarpacie, a hilly region on the slopes of the Carpathian mountains, used to be a very poor region. But in the mid-19th century it cherished hopeful moments for a great future ... An apothecary from Lvov, Ignacy Łukasiewicz constructed the first kerosene lamp in 1853 and then founded a distillation plant of crude oil, one of the first distillation plants in the world, in Ulaszowice near Jasło. Unfortunately, the region did not become a Polish Kuwait. It remained poor and many of its inhabitants travelled to America in search of work. Close relations between those who emigrated to the USA and those who remained in Poland remain lively. Many regions of the former Galicia (this was the name of Małopolska under Austrian rule) still function thanks to dollars flowing from the other side of the Ocean.

Tourists may be interested in old aristocratic residences in Baranów, Łańcut, Krasiczyn, Wiśnicz and in other places. Most of them have been adapted as museums.

The most tragic place in the history of Poland is located in the Podkarpacie region near Oświęcim. Millions of people come to visit it in order to pay tribute to their relatives and friends murdered by the Nazis in the concentration camp of Auschwitz-Birkenau (Oświęcim-Brzezinka). Over a million people, mainly Jews and Poles, from several dozen countries lost their lives there.

Wadowice is one of the typical towns of the Podkarpacie. Karol Wojtyła, otherwise known as Pope John Paul II, was born there.

This region is famous for its beer and salt. Beer made in Żywiec and Okocim wins the competition with the most famous brands of beer all over the world. Wieliczka, on the other hand, is famous as a unique monument of the mining art: a salt mine going back as far as the 9th century. In the old excavations miners carved in salt wonderful chambers and chapels adorned with sculptures. There is also an underground sanatorium where illnesses of the respiratory track and various allergies are treated.

The extraction of salt is still continued on a small scale. The mine is visited by millions of tourists who admire the underground, mysterious and beautiful world with bated breath.

Polish Uplands

A long time ago, about 80 or even 200 thousand years ago, in the Paleolithic period, the oldest inhabitants of Poland lived in caves, of course. Vestiges of their presence are to be seen near Kraków, Zawiercie and in the limestone caves at Ojców.

About five or six thousand years ago, a big industrial center was established in Krzemionki Opatowskie. Flint used in producing tools of all kinds was excavated there. The demand was big because people needed tools and weapons in order to survive. The axes were even bought by tribes living in the area of the Elbe river in Germany. These archaic mines constitute an interesting monument of human enterpreneurship in prehistoric times and are open to tourists.

In the 18th century, Staropolskie Zagłębie, an industrial center, was founded there. It was the cradle of contemporary industry in Poland.

However, the biggest industrial center is located in Upper Silesia. Avoid this region unless you have business there! Or perhaps you're interested to see what the Ruhr or the French departments of Nord and Pas-de-Calais, or old mining centers in middle England were like many years ago. Poland has not yet gotten rid of the old coal mines, iron steel works and coking plants which constitute the basis of the Silesian industry and the greatest hazard to the enivironment. They continue to function and only the most harmful or exploited ones are being closed. Constituting three per cent of the total area of Poland, the Katowice voivodship* supplies one-fifth of the gross national industrial product. Air pollution exceeds accepted levels and threatens nature not to mention the health of people living there. Parts of Silesia are like a wasteland, a lunar landscape in fact. Tourists have nothing to look for there. Unless it's the desert they are looking for. A unique region of shifting sands some 30 square kilometers in area is called the Błędowska desert. There are no camels there, but one can certainly see a mirage. Częstochowa, the site of the famous sanctuary of the Holy Virgin on Jasna Góra, lies to the north of Upper Silesia. No other city in Poland has attracted so many tourist–pilgrims from Poland and abroad for so many centuries. The cult of St. Mary, which is centered on the monastery of the Paulite Fathers in Jasna Góra with its miraculous picture of the Holy Virgin, is of special importance to Polish Catholicism. The monastery survived the siege of the Swedish army in 1655 and played on important role in the history of Poland. Between Częstochowa and Kraków there is a long chain of limestone hills called the Krakowsko-Częstochowska Upland. It is full of picturesque rocky forms and numerous caves (not all penetrated by speleologists yet). Ruins of old castles occupy the tops of some of the hills. These are the so-called ,,Eagles' Nests" which are a favorite trail with tourists. The rocks near Ojców in the Prądnik valley are not only beatiful but serve young amateurs of mountaineering as a place to practice mountain climbing. Some of them go on to become alpinists, and Polish Himalaya mountain climbers are among the best in the world. The Polish conquerors of Mount Everest and K-2 took their first steps in the Prądnik valley...

We are very close to Cracow now. If a visitor had just enough time to visit one city of Poland, it should be Cracow. The Old Town, mostly 14th century in date, has preserved with slight changes the Medieval urban layout; with its fragments of walls and fortificiations it constitutes a rarity in Poland. In the 19th century some of the walls were removed and the moats filled forming a wide green belt called the Planty which surrounds the historic center of

---

* A voivodship is an administration unit. There are 49 voivodships in Poland

the city. Buildings from past ages have been preserved: churches, palaces, houses and the royal castle on Wawel hill. It owes its Renaissance shape to Florentine architects from the first half of the 16th century, but the foundations of the castle are earlier – Gothic and even Pre-Romanesque and Romanesque.

There is a kernel of truth in the legends connected with Cracow. Propably a century or two before the birth of Poland, Cracow was already an important town, the abode of "a strong" pagan prince mentioned in the legend describing the life of the saints Cyril and Methodius. The prince reigned over the Vistulanie tribe and continued to "harm" Christians in spite of warnings to change his behavior. So he was baptized by force „in a foreign land", which was probably Moravia, a powerful country at the time.

Another legend associated with Cracow is that about Krak, founder of Cracow, and his daughter Wanda, who not wanting to marry a German threw herself into the Vistula. To pay homage to the father and daughter, two mounds were made over a thousand years ago. Perhaps they really were the tombs of rulers or a cult place of the pagan peoples. In folk fantasy Krak had a terrible enemy – a dragon who lived in a cave under Wawel hill and devoured beatiful virgins. The dragon was killed by a cunning shoemaker who treated the beast to a special dish: a sheepskin stuffed with sulfur and tar. After such a meal the dragon could not quench his thirst; he drank and drank water from the Vistula until he had drank more than half and then he burst.

Another legend from Cracow is related to the Tartar invasion in the 13th century. The "Lajkonik" which every year during the Days of Cracow runs through the streets is something akin to a centaur but dressed in oriental clothes. An hourly bugle-call is played even today from the tower of the St. Mary Church. The bugle-call breaks off in the middle of a note because it is said that the medieval trumpeter was pierced through the throat by a Tartar's arrow while playing.

In the mid-11th century Cracow became the capital of Poland. During the feudal period it was the abode of the Senior of all the princes. Upon reunification, Casimir the Great, the last king of the Piast dynasty, established an Academy in 1364. It is the second oldest university in Central Europe (after the University in Prague), older than any university in Germany. Today the Jagiellonian University pays tribute to its benefactor from the dynasty following the Piast kings, and it is still famous all over the world.

In the 16th century, considered the golden age in Poland, not many European cities could vie with Cracow in the pace of developing construction and commerce, culture and science. Vestiges of the times are to be seen first of all in Wawel, in the castle and cathedral neighboring it, the coronation-place of Polish kings. In its vault the most eminent Poles continue to be buried even nowadays. The Royal and Cathedral Treasuries contain precious church and national masterpieces of art such as the coronation regalia and spear of St. Maurice granted to Bolesław the Brave by the German Emperor Otto III. The castle chambers contain precious paintings and one of the best colletions of tapestries, the so-called "Wawel arrases". The Sigismund bell in the tower of the Cathedral is 8 meters in circumference and sounds on days special to Poland.

While the majestic Wawel is lofty in character, the main Market continues to be the parlor of Cracow. Its chief adornment, the Sukiennice, a long market hall of the 14th century, beautifully reconstructed in the Renaissance style. Equally important is the Gothic brick-and-stone St. Mary Church with two high towers, each crowned in a different way. A Gothic altar (13 x 11 metres) made by Wit Stwosz, who lived in Cracow and Nuremberg, is a real treasure. The small Romanesque Church of St. Wojciech was erected at the turn of the 12th century.

The Wierzynek restaurant is located in one of the buildings in the central market. In 1364 a townsman and councilor, Mikołaj Wierzynek, received monarchs who came to Kraków at the invitation of the Polish king Casimir the Great: emperor Charles IV, Hungarian King

Louis, Danish King Waldemar IV, Cyprus King Peter, Brandenburg margrave Otto, as well as princes Casimir of Szczecin and Ziemowit Mazowiecki. The banquet lasted three days, but the monarchs enjoyed themselves so much that they forgot why they had come to Cracow. The Crusades against the Turks were not organized and the idea to integrate Central Europe in face of a common danger failed. The situation has not changed much since then.

The Museum of the Czartoryski Princes possesses two masterpieces of European painting: *The Portrait of Cecilia Gallerani* (which used to be called *Lady with the Ermine*) by Leonardo da Vinci (experts claim that this painting is as good as the famous *Gioconda*), and Rembrandt's *A Landscape with the Good Samaritan*.

Cracow is not only a museum of a city. It is also the center of Polish contemporary art, just like Warsaw is. Taking into consideration all these facts, it is hardly surprising that the inhabitants of Cracow detest King Sigismund III Vasa for moving the capital of Poland from Cracow to Warsaw. They claim he did it illegally and they still have hopes that somebody will do something about it sometime in the future...

Several kilometres to the north of Cracow there are relatively low chains of the very old Świętokrzyskie Mountains. Forests cover the slopes, including the famous Fir Wood, described by many Polish writers. Unfortunately, the neighboring cement plants are polluting it extensively. The Świętokrzyski National Park is also in danger.

One of its highest peaks, called Łysa Góra, was once believed to be the gathering place of witches. This legend probably originated in olden times, when there was a pagan cult center there. In order to chase the witches away and to uproot old beliefs, Benedictine monks constructed a monastery on the top of the mountain called Saint Cross at the end of the 12th century. At the end of the 19th century, it was transformed into a prison of ill repute. At present, part of the monastery is used by nuns and in the other part there is a museum.

The Małopolska and Lubelska Uplands are separated by the Vistula river, very picturesque in this part and preserved almost in the same state in which it used to be centuries ago. Inland sailors (almost non-existent by now) are worried about it, but lovers of nature, especially of water fowl living in the neighboring meadows and sandy islands in the river, can admire the landscape. Out of the whole one-thousand-kilometer long Vistula river, this part is the most beautiful.

Tourists can visit two small towns on the river, which used to make money on the cereal trade Sandomierz with its Romanesque, Gothic, Renaissance and Baroque monuments and Kazimierz Dolny beloved by painters. In Warsaw artistic circles it is a popular pastime to go to the beautiful market in Kazimierz from time to time. It is even better to possess a house there. The vicinity of Kazimierz can be characterized as an area of deep canyons in soft chalk, covered with a fertile layer of loess and thickets.

Lublin is the biggest city in the Lubelska Upland. It is also the biggest city east of the Vistula river. It played the role of the Polish capital twice in history: during several days after the First World War and during several months after the Second World War. It is a very old city whose first settlements were discovered to date as far back as the 9th century or even perhaps the 8th century. The most precious monument of the Old Town in Lublin is located in the Holy Trinity Chapel in the Castle. It is a wall painting made in the Russian and Byzantine tradition. It was given to Lublin by King Władysław Jagiełło in 1385. The king was a Lithuanian and had a sentiment for the artistic style of Ruthenia which remained under the influence of the Grand Duchy of Lithuania.

Zamość, much smaller than Lublin and located to the south of it, is considered to be the pearl of the Renaissance. The town was built in a very peculiar way: it was founded in 1580 by the Royal Chancellor Jan Zamoyski in an empty field according to plans designed by Bernardo Morando, an Italian architect who also supervised the construction. The town received an original Town Hall with features of Mannerism and Baroque, while some tenements were adorned in the Armenian style. Zamość is a favorite town among settlers from Armenia who come to Catholic Poland in considerable numbers.

To the south of Zamość there is the Roztocze hill chain, covered with forests and few human settlements. It is crossed by numerous deep canyons. Nature has survived here, even after the heavy fighting of the Second World War when Roztocze was a center of the Polish underground army and an area from which the German forces attempted to deport a hundred thousand Poles living there in order to give the fertile land to German settlers. The guerrillas managed to prevent the Nazis from sending Polish children away to Germany to germanize then.

Roztocze constitutes the southeastern border of the Polish Uplands, but it continues farther into Ukraine, up to Lvov, one of the most eminent Polish towns in the eastern part of the Republic of Poland, a country which used to comprise many nations within its frontiers once. But today it is a closed chapter in history. At present Poland is ethnically almost a homogenous country and all the national minorities constitute not more than three or four per cent of all inhabitants.

Sudety and the Silesian Lowland

The region is composed of two different parts: a mountain chain belonging to the old Czech Massif and the Silesian Plain along the Oder river which is a fragment of the big Middle European Lowland. Only history joins these two parts together creating the historical land of Silesia characterized by a complicated and often dramatic past.

A thousand years ago, there lived several tribes of which the Ślężanie were the biggest. They had their great religious and sacrificial center on the solitary mountain called Ślęża or Sobótka, while power was probably located in a town on the site of the present Wrocław. Apart from the Polanie who initiated the creation of the Polish state, and the Vistulan tribe who had appeared in history much earlier but without success, the Ślężanie were the framework of the Polish nation. Some time later (and not for long) the Pomeranians were incorporated into the new state, while the Mazovians had a looser relation with Poland for several centuries more.

In the reign of the first Piast rulers, German attempts to rule over Silesia, which used to lead all the other Polish regions in development, were successfully repelled. Wrocław was a big center of crafts and commerce, and it had a bishop since the year 1000. Several monastic orders settled in Silesia, first of all the Cistercian monks who brought colonists from the West, mostly from Germany. In the Sudety mountains copper, iron, stannum, and even gold were excavated! Even today there are adventurers trying to find gold dust in rivers in Silesia like in the Clondike.

During the 12th century, Silesia not only became an independent duchy, but was quickly broken up into smaller duchies. The Czechs took advantage of the situation to impose their protectorate over all of Silesia.

But before the Czech conquest, Silesia faced an invasion by... the Mongols. In 1241 Polish knights were defeated in a battle near Legnica. Prince Henry the Pious died, but the Mongols' march towards the west was stopped. For the first time Poland played its role of rampart of Christendom.

In spite of Silesia's dependency upon the Czechs, most inhabitants spoke Polish. Old commercial and family bonds were preserved. When in 1526 Silesia and the Czechs came under the rule of the Habsburgs from Austria, germanization processes were intensified. Only in the eastern part of Silesia, near Opole and Upper Silesia (geographically belonging to the Polish Uplands) did feelings of Polishhood remain strong.

In 1763, Silesia passed under the authority of Prussia which was even more determined to destroy Polishhood. Fortunately, without success. In the period between the two world wars, after Poland regained its independence, the majority of inhabitants of the Opole region belonging to Germany considered themselves to be Polish and spoke the Silesian dialect at home.

After the Second World War, all of Silesia, apart from a small part belonging to Czechoslovakia, was returned to Poland. Most Germans fled to Germany during the final stage of the war or were deported. About a million autochthons of an unspecified national status remained there. Under German rule they considered themselves to be Poles, but when Poland started to govern there, many of them preferred to be Germans. Other autochthons (living in Upper Silesia which used to be Polish before) started to describe themselves as Silesians.

With the overthrow of the communist regime, the Germans living in Silesia obtained the status of a national minority. Many of them emigrated to Germany. Others have accepted the present situation, elected their own deputies to the Parliament of the Republic of Poland and are cooperating with the Poles better and better, even though pressures and disputes common wherever different nationalities live together come to the fore from time to time.

Lower Silesia, almost totally depopulated after the war, was settled by Polish citizens from all parts of Poland, mainly from the territories east of the Bug river which Poland lost to the USSR. Many former emigrants who had left Poland earlier for France and Westphalia in search of work, came back to Silesia. Most of them settled in Wałbrzych, a mining city on the slopes of the Sudety mountains and this is why the French language can be heard in the streets in some districts! Polish emigrants from other countries also came there: from Bosnia, Rumania and Canada. Ukrainians from the Bieszczady mountains and some Lemks from the lower Beskidy were resettled here. Some of them returned home at a later date, but some remained in Silesia. Several thousand Greeks and Macedonians, usually political emigrants fleeing the civil strife in Greece, came there. Nowhere else in Poland can one encounter such a melting pot of nationalities, but, fortunately, the process of integration was surprisingly quick. The new inhabitants of Lower Silesia, dominated mainly by young people, are characterized by a dynamic and ardent local patriotism.

This is especially visible in Wrocław. This big city was transformed at the order of Hitler into the Festung Breslau fortress at the end of the Second World War. The German garrison of the city-stronghold held out until the fall of the Third Reich. Whole districts were totally demolished and losses were up to 70 percent of the urban buildings. The Old Town was almost completely burned out. Its main pride was the Town Hall, a priceless monument of Gothic public architecture. The complex of churches and monasteries, which used to be called a small Vatican, did not suffer so much. It was located on a former island on the Oder river, the site of the oldest settlements dating a thousand years back.

The Baroque buildings of Wrocław University were left intact. Following the war, professors from Lvov, which was no longer inside the new Polish borders, started lecturing there. Although former residents of Lvov constituted only a part of the new inhabitants, they imbued Wrocław with a special character and imposed big city traditions and cultural preferences on the much more numerous village and small town population.

In ten years the monuments of Wrocław were mostly restored and the young population changed the city's status from a deep province to the third capital of Poland (just behind Warsaw and Cracow). It was a real sociological miracle which became the topic of many scientific theses. The Wrocław mathematics school which continued the traditions of its counterpart from Lvov, highly esteemed during the interwar years, achieved a worldwide reputation. The Polish electronic industry was born in Wrocław, including the Elwro computers factory. The experimental theater-laboratory of Jerzy Grotowski gained international fame in the 1960s. The modern pantomime of Henryk Tomaszewski was also very popular.

Wrocław is a city of fantasy, with many artistic events and original street holidays taking place frequently. This was especially obvious during martial law. Young people had illegal organizations all over Poland, but only in Wrocław did they start to fight against the communists with laughter. They invented the Orange Alternative: street manifestations, apparently totally apolitical and constituting a combination of the fashionable happening with a theater of Medieval goliards. Once they paraded through Wrocław in the red hoods of brownies (because brownies also lead underground lives!); another time they dressed up as policemen and stopped each other to help the beloved authorities persecuting Solidarity activists. Yet another time crowds of young people stood in front of the main police station and sang that they also wanted to be imprisoned. The Communist authorities did not know whether to pretend nothing was happening or to laugh with everybody else.

There are many other interesting towns rich in monuments in Lower Silesia. Świdnica, where Piast princes opposed the Czechs the longest, was called a small Cracow because of the numerous old churches. There are Piast castles (some only in ruins and some fully reconstructed) in Bolków, Ząbkowice, Chojnów and other towns. Legnica takes pride in various religious and secular buildings in the Gothic, Renaissance and Baroque styles. There are many aristocratic residences, usually in the Baroque style. Lubiąż attracts tourists thanks to the gigantic Baroque building of the Cistercian abbey, even bigger than Wawel and resembling the Escorial near Madrid in architecture. A similar and equally beautiful Cistercian abbey can be seen in Henryków. Trzebnica can boast of a lovely Cistercian convent constructed in 1202. Walls from the Middle Ages and a Gothic and Renaissance town hall, as well as Renaissance burghers' houses, are still to be seen in Lwówek Śląski. Oleśnica is famous for its beautiful skyline of church towers and defensive turrets.

Tourists looking for shivers and adventure can go to Lubiąż, the castle in Książ near Wałbrzych and to a huge stronghold in Srebrna Góra constructed in the 18th century. Under all these constructions there are allegedly labyrinths of underground passages made by Nazi prisoners who were later shot. What had been hidden there? Perhaps precious museum collections plundered from Wrocław? Perhaps a factory of V-2 missiles? Or perhaps the famous Amber Chamber? From time to time new ideas appear but it is difficult to penetrate the mysterious passages.

It is also worthwhile to visit Lubin which 25 years ago was a small, poor and forgotten town. Today it is the capital of a copper extraction center which is one of the biggest in the world. Copper deposits were discovered by Polish geologists (in German times there were a few small mines in this region). Copper export constitutes one of the pillars of Polish economy. Unfortunately, copper processing at works in Legnica and Głogów contaminates the environment considerably.

Śląsk Opolski also possesses many tourist towns, first of all Opole with a 14th century castle of the Piast dynasty, a Gothic cathedral and the Town Hall which was built in 1936, but which is a copy of Palazzo Vecchio in Florence. Guests in Opole are attracted more by annual Festivals of Polish Songs rather than by the monuments. The festivals have been organized for almost 30 years now. The prince's palace in Brzeg is considered to be the most beautiful monument of Renaissance architecture in Poland. Nysa is also rich in architectural monuments. The town was part of the estates of Wrocław bishops, but it always maintained close relations with Poland. Two Polish kings, Michał Korybut Wiśniowiecki and Jan Sobieski, were educated there in the 17th century. Paczków, surrounded by a wall with 19 turrets and towers, is called (perhaps exaggeratedly) the Polish Carcassone, while Prudnik attempts to be the Polish Verone. It does have the subtle beauty and climate of Italian towns. The Sudety mountains are the biggest tourist attraction in Śląsk. Strange mountains, they are a collection of individual chains and massifs, separated by dales or deep river valleys and streams. Almost every peak has a unique geological construction and appearance.

The Sudety mountains are 300 km long and 50 km wide and separate Poland and the Czech Republic. Their highest part is constituted by the Karkonosze, flattened table-like mountains with one mountain similar to a volcano, Śnieżka (1601 m), rising higher. The Karkonosze are covered with rocky rubble which makes them look like old mountains, changed by glaciers and erosion. On the other hand, picturesque rocky potholes, hanging valleys, small lakes and strange rocky forms, such as jags, turrets, mushrooms, clubs and even shapes of elephants or perhaps dinosaurs were created.

On the slopes of the Karkonosze numerous holiday resorts are located. Karpacz and

Szklarska Poręba are the most famous ones and are visited by many guests from Germany. Snow lies long in the year and skiing routes are very diversified, although hardly challenging to regular visitors from the Alps. But does everybody have to win the Olympic Games?

The Stołowe mountains are still more peculiar. Seen from a distance, they may seem to be an almost ideal plateau, but after one approaches closer, they turn out to be a strange stone labyrinth in which it is possible to walk for hours on end. The Sowie mountains are not impressing in any way, but they are of special importance to geologists: they are the oldest mountains in Poland, formed as far back as the Archaic period.

Until recently the gentle slopes of the Izerskie mountains were described as a beautiful and wooded area where the popular health resort of Świeradów is located. The mountains today are bare the forests having been devastated by acid rains and pollution from factories in neighboring Czech Republic and Germany as well as from Polish factories.

Jelenia Góra plays the role of capital of the Sudety mountains. It is located in a valley between four mountain chains. Once the city was famous in Europe for textiles of the highest qualities. The burghers and especially the weavers in Jelenia Góra were wealthy and rather ambitious, so the city owes to them some wonderful churches, palaces and houses constructed between the late Middle Ages and the 19th century. Remnants of the old constructions have been preserved and have been renovated and reconstructed.

Kłodzko plays a less important role in the eastern regions of the Sudety. Long the object of rivalry between Poles and Czechs, it was where 14th century monks wrote the famous Florian Psalter, one of the oldest monuments of the Polish language. The Czechs claim, on the other hand, that the architecture of the city, especially its Gothic bridge, is an imitation of constructions in Prague. The Prussian King Frederick II solved the Slavic dispute by erecting a huge stronghold over the city. Its multilevel underground passages are the object of fiction stories, which perhaps are more than just fiction.

It is very close from Kłodzko to health resorts famous already in the 19th century (their specialty – oxalate waters): Polanica, Kudowa and Duszniki, where 16-year-old Frederick Chopin used to give concerts.

In the caves of the Sudety mountains, the old abandoned mines and rocky precipices, gem hunters look for loot. It's always a fashionable hobby! Sometimes they find beautiful nephrites, amethysts, opals and other semi-precious stones. Nature was not favorable to Poland in terms of precious stones, but even the semi-precious ones shine beautifully in jewelry, which has become a real art in Poland. The jewels are mainly of silver, not gold. Not many Poles know that Poland has considerable deposits of silver! Silver is obtained, for example, as a by-product from the processing of copper excavated in Silesia.

Wielkopolska Lowland

The neighboring Wielkopolska is totally different. There are no mountains and the land is mostly flat although dotted with hills. Wielkopolska is part of the big Central European Plain. There are rather few natural resources: salt, brown coal and sand for the glass industry, as well as some natural gas. The soil is rather poor.

The history of this region was hardly easy, but less dramatic than in other parts of Poland. Wielkopolska is not famous for the dash of its inhabitants. The people are considered to be reliable, honest, good working and serious. They are pedantic, sometimes even boring according to people from Warsaw, Cracow or Wrocław. Nevertheless, everybody is jealous of their orderliness and wealth. It is the best developed district in Poland.

When one comes to Wielkopolska from Germany, one may not notice any difference at all in the appearance of towns or the quality of service. The only difference is the lack of a highway (which is in the works). On the other hand, entering Wielkopolska from other districts of Poland, one may notice at once that fields are in a better condition, houses are nicer, the service in shops and restaurants more friendly, and there are no holes in the streets. Truly the West! Only the Warta river could be a bit cleaner! (It is Wielkopolska's main river). But then the Rhine, Seine and Mosel rivers are not the cleanest rivers in the world, either.

Wielkopolska was not a wild wood even in Roman times. Five centuries before Christ the pre-Slavic culture of the Lusatians flourished here with Biskupin being its best representation. It is an island stronghold, composed of over one hundred rather prosperous houses, located along 13 regular streets and surrounded by a stockade. A 120-meter-long bridge connected the settlement with the mainland. Fragments of wooden constructions were preserved in the swampy soil and were reconstructed to a considerable degree so that tourists can imagine what the life of their ancestors was like.

In the first centuries after Christ, the amber route crossed Wielkopolska leading from the Mediterranean to the Baltic Sea. Roman ladies liked jewelry made of amber, while rich Romans used amber to decorate furniture and even walls. The amber route went on to an ancient settlement (or perhaps a Roman stronghold?) called Calisia by Ptolemy in the second century after Christ. Most probably the legendary Kruszwica on the Gopło lake was also on the amber route. The bad king Popiel used to live there. According to a legend, he was eaten by mice. The story presumably refers to strife in the 9th century between the Polanie and Goplanie tribes, and the victorious Polanie were probably the mice which ate Popiel. They were headed by prince Mieszko I who started to unite all the Polish tribes. He succeeded by force, an accepted way of succeeding at the time, and still tolerated nowadays.

Kruszwica was forgotten. To wipe away the tears it has its Mice Tower, a vestige of the 14th century castle, somewhat leaning but not as much as the tower in Pisa.

Gniezno was the first capital of Poland. In the 10th century it had about 4000 inhabitants. Poznań was the same size. It played the role of a capital together with Gniezno. Bolesław, the Brave the first king of Poland, took care of both towns: in 968 Poznań became the seat of a bishop and in 1000 Gniezno, was turned into a metropolitan see. The archbishop of Gniezno is still the first among equals due to the seniority of this metropolis. The cathedral in Gniezno, erected in the 14th century in the Gothic style, can also boast of an earlier Romanesque monument: the famous bronze doors with a bas-relief depicting scenes from the life of St. Adalbert who baptized the Prussians. The door, made probably by masters from Lorraine, is considered a masterpiece of European art.

The cathedral in Poznań is still older. At first it was a wooden pre-Romanesque basilica, but in the 11th century it was reconstructed first in the Romanesque, and later in the Gothic style. But that's not all! Its interior decorations were influenced by the Renaissance and Baroque style. The facade changed according to the Classicist style, while the Golden Chapel, mausoleum of the founders of the Polish state, was reconstructed at the beginning of the 19th century. At present its interiors are in the Byzantine style. Thus all architectural styles present in Poland have been intermixed here. Unfortunately, the cathedral was seriously damaged in 1945. The last reconstruction returned it to its Gothic appearance.

Poznań, a wealthy city from olden times, features sound and massive architecture, but it also has several buildings which are surprisingly light in the Renaissance style, particulary the beautiful Town Hall resembling the best Italian models. It is richly adorned with loggias and surmounted with an attic, while its facade is covered with wall paintings and graffiti. At the turn of the 19th century, when Poznań came under Prussian authority, the aristocracy living in Wielkopolska reconstructed its palaces in the fashionable Classicist style. Some of these families supported the Polish national spirit by founding libraries and art collections which have given rise to contemporary museums.

Poznań is better known as a city of Mercury and not Apollo. St. John's Fairs were held already in the 15th century. The annual International Poznań Fairs have continued the tradition since the 1920s. The fairs are important to businessmen from all over the world. Poznań is an important industrial center with the heavy industry in first place – the H. Cegielski factory producing mainly railway equipment. In 1956 Poznań, considered to be an apolitical and calm city, faced mass demonstrations and workers riots. The rebellion was put down bloodily becoming the talk of the day. Memory of the victims has remained.

But it is all history now. At present Poznań is a city where life proceeds sedately, without drama.

Poznań residents have many attractions waiting for them in the city's environs. Sailors have several lakes at their disposal. Amateurs of forests can go to the Wielkopolski National Park, the botanical garden which is the biggest in Poland and which surrounds the palace in Kórnik famous for its collection of art objects, and the park near the palace in Rogalin where there are almost a thousand majestic oaks. The biggest ones, called Lech, Czech and Rus, have up to 9 metres in circumference!

Strzelno is worth visiting among the smaller towns in Wielkopolska. It is a real treasury of Romanesque architecture represented, for example, by the abbey complex built in the 12th century, a church from the same period with original sculptured columns and a small church of St. Procopius, one of the most obvious Romanesque constructions. Gostynin boasts a Baroque church from the end of the 17th century, similar to Santa Maria della Salute in Venice. Leszno is famous for temples of the Czech fathers, supporters of Jan Hus, who were expelled from Bohemia and Moravia and found shelter in Gostynin, where they founded one of the most important cultural centers in Europe. The famous scientist and pedagogue, Jan Amos Komensky, was the rector of the Academy there.

Two regions, which are similar geographically but very distinct historically, are neighbors of Wielkopolska: Ziemia Lubuska on the west and Kujawy on the northeast.

The Piasts lost Ziemia Lubuska very early to Brandenburg. The region is located at the junction of the Oder and Warta rivers. It is separated from Wielkopolska by a peculiar river called Obra which sometimes flows north and sometimes south, depending on the water level in the two big rivers it connects. It is a rare example of a bifurcation. Zielona Góra is the capital of Ziemia Lubuska. It is famous for vineyards cultivated only in this part of Poland. They do not provide much wine, and the wine is not of high quality, but the tradition is preserved for the benefit of tourists. There are little attractions, although Ziemia Lubuska belongs to the afforested part of Poland and abounds in lakes. It is still virgin land.

Kujawy lie along the left bank of the Vistula river and are rather scarcely wooded. As the very name indicates, the famous Polish folk dance called "kujawiak" orginated here; it is melodious and sentimental, and renders the mood of the region. Inowrocław, famous for its saline waters used for medical and industrial purposes alike, as well as Włocławek, where there is a great dam on the Vistula river, are its main cities. A big artificial lagoon where water sports are practiced was created thanks to this dam.

Small Ciechocinek is still more famous. Together with Krynica it is the most famous health resort in Poland. It was founded at the beginning of the 19th century by the eminent scientist and writer of the Enlightenment era, Stanisław Staszic. The iodine filling the air near the gradation towers down which the saline waters flow cures respiratory aliments.

Unfortunately, a contrary influence upon the lungs is exercised by the air pollution from the electrical power station in Konin which uses deposits of brown coal. A dropping watertable and resulting drying-out of meadows and peat bogs, and the disappearance of wooded areas are an even more important danger to the natural advantages of Kujawy and southern part of Wielkopolska. Flora and even fauna typical of the steppes have appeared in many places. Fortunately lions have not been sighted yet.

Łódź, the second biggest city in Poland, is located to the east of the Wielkopolska Lowland, at its border with Mazovia and the Polish Uplands. It has almost one million inhabitants. The city was founded more than a hundred years ago as a center of the textile industry. If one holds a competition for the ugliest city in Poland, Łódź has probably the best chance to win. But even this city has an attraction for foreign tourists: The Filming Academy considered to be one of the best filming academies in the world. Who has not heard about Andrzej Wajda, Krzysztof Zanussi, Kszysztof Kieślowski and Roman Polański?

The landscape of Mazovia is the quintessence of Poland. Spacious fields and meadows, willows, pine forests spotted with white birches, a melancholic air lost in thought... This Poland was loved by Frederick Chopin who was born in Żelazowa Wola, not far away from Warsaw. This picture was preserved in his heart when he left Poland and this mood is ever present in his musical masterpieces. This apparently dull and monotonous landscape, which becomes interesting in autumn when trees are covered with colorful leaves and in winter when white snow lies everywhere, was painted by numerous Polish painters. But that was a long time ago.

Nowadays, when traditional, idyllic villages have almost disappeared, and town-like constructions have arisen everywhere, the old Mazovia has ceased to exist.

The capital of Poland is located in a place devoid of any special natural beauty. Warsaw itself is the only attraction.

Its attraction is not in the beauty of its architecture nor the original urban designs. Of course, parts of it can be compared to the most beautiful capitals in the world. The rest is rather coincidental, mainly because it is the result of circumstances, the ambitions of kings and nobles, the wartime damages, the will to reconstruct it as it used to be, important housing needs, lack of financial means and the communist regime's obsession to build a truly socialistic city. Recently, there is the ambition to give Warsaw the outside appearance of a modern Western metropoly. Put together, these factors have created urban chaos.

In spite of this, Warsaw is an interesting city with a character of its own, a city which many foreigners fall in love with, even those coming from more beautiful cities.

Its coat of arms is also very appropriate: A mermaid, strange creature which it is, half a scaly fish and half a beautiful naked girl with a sword raised courageously. Ugliness, beauty and determination. All in one...

Warsaw has been called the Invincible City. It has been called: Heart of Poland.

And now some history. When Poznań, Gniezno, Cracow and Sandomierz were already towns famous all over Europe, Warsaw did not yet exist. Only on the right bank of the Vistula river, on the site of the modern Bródno housing district, there was a small settlement protecting the river crossing. At the end of the 13th century Warsaw was founded on the site of the present Old Town. It took quite a long time for Warsaw to gain in importance. Even in Mazovia there were other, more important towns: Czersk, Płock and Grójec.

The union of Poland and Lithuania at the end of the 14th century, and first of all the recovered access to the sea, started its great career. Commercial tracks led via Warsaw towards Lithuania, and pinewood rafts loaded with cereals drifted down the Vistula towards the Baltic Sea. The goods were later sold profitably in Western Europe. At the end of the 16th century Mazovia was finally annexed to Poland and a union with Lithuania was signed. When king Sigismund III Vasa, who also dreamt of recovering the Swedish throne, took power, Warsaw became the capital and started to develop rapidly located as it was in the center of the state and much closer to the Baltic sea than Cracow was.

Leaner years came in the mid-17th century. Numerous wars, especially the Swedish deluge, which destroyed Warsaw, caused a standstill in its development, and in the 18th century a political and economic breakdown. During the reign of the last Polish king Stanislaus August, during the Enlightenment, Warsaw returned to its former glory and received new and beautiful buildings. However, the rule of Stanislaus Augustus was the end of the state. Poland was partitioned and lost independence in 1795.

A year earlier the insurrection led by Tadeusz Kościuszko was defeated. Warsaw people headed by the shoemaker Jan Kilinski participated in it. Another tragic event which took place was the massacre of Praga (part of Warsaw located on the left bank of the Vistula river) by the Tsarist general Suvorov.

During the Napoleonic age Warsaw (capital of the ephemereal Duchy of Warsaw) attempted to regain independence for all of the Polish regions. In vain.

Mazovia and Podlasie Lowland

The November Uprising broke out in 1830 in Warsaw. A year later it ended with the conquest of Warsaw by general Paskiewicz. A French minister Sebastiani said the famous sentence: "L'ordre regne a Varsovie". Yes, the order of terror and oppression came back. In 1863 another uprising was organized there. It has come to be known as the January Uprising. Direct fighting did not occur in Warsaw, but many Warsaw inhabitants died in the uprising or were sent into exile in Siberia.

1905: The fourth uprising connected with a social revolution. Warsaw was again bloodied. Thousands of inhabitants died on the gallows and in exile in Siberia.

Finally the most tragic act.

1939: Warsaw fervently opposed Hitler's aggression. It fought, completely deserted by its allies for three weeks.

1943: A heroic uprising of the Jews imprisoned in the Warsaw ghetto which ended in its complete destruction.

1944: The great Warsaw Uprising lasting 63 days and engaging several divisions of the German Army. At that time the Red Army was in right-bank Warsaw and did not offer any help. About 180,000 Poles died, mainly civilians. Three-fourths of the buildings were destroyed by bombs, fires, and finally, the constructions which survived were systematically blown up by the Germans.

The communist government took care to reconstruct historic districts during the first years after the war. Everything of value in Warsaw was reconstructed. At times it was even more beautiful than it used to be before the war, because many monuments lacked proper documentation and were reconstructed according to paintings by Bernardo Bellotto called Canaletto, who made detailed portraits of Warsaw streets in the 18th century.

Thus the Old Town is really quite new but it does not differ from the Old Town in which Poles lived two or three hundred years ago. Krakowskie Przedmieście starts at the Royal Castle. It is undoubtedly one of the most beautiful streets in the world, with an irregular course, elegant palaces (most of them in the Classicist style), churches and houses. Its continuation is the Nowy Świat street, shaped like a gentle arc and lined with town houses. It is a really beautiful fragment of the city. The last part of the Royal Road is the Aleje Ujazdowskie lined with trees and serving as a summertime Warsaw corso. Aleje Ujazdowskie end with the Classicist Belvedere palace .

The huge park of Łazienki is full of old trees, ponds and canals; it is mosly in the English style with fragments in the French garden style. The palace complex was designed by king Stanislaus Augustus. The spacious and similarly beautiful park of Paderewski is located on the other side of the Vistula river. It may not be modest, but the Parisian Luxembourg or Tuilleries, as well as Hyde Park in London seem to be rather rickety in comparison Warsaw Łazienki.

The monumental building of the Grand Theater (opera and ballet) is considered to be one of the tourist attractions in Warsaw. It was designed by Antonio Corazzi and is a masterpiece of the Classicist style. There is also the Baroque palace of Krasiński designed by Tylman van Gameren. There is one more Baroque palace on the outskirts of Warsaw, Wilanów. It was the residence of king Jan Sobieski, the King who saved Vienna from the Turks in 1683. The palace is a division of the National Museum whose main building is located in the city center. A few words should be said about the peculiarity of the Palace of Culture and Science, a towering 234 m erected by Joseph Stalin as a gift of the Soviet nations and called the dream of a drunken pastry-cook by Warsaw inhabitants. It does resemble in shape a gigantic layer cake. Nobody knows what to do with this troublesome gift, especially that in spite of its ugliness, it has blended into the landscape of the city, just like the Eiffel tower in Paris. There are few monuments on the outskirts of Warsaw. One should mention the huge Citadel in Żoliborz, constructed at the order of the Russian tsar in order to hold tight reins on the insurgent city, as well as the Powązki cemetery, a monumental necropoly where the most eminent Poles have been buried for over two centuries.

There is not much more to see. Most tourists prefer cultural life to monuments; they want to get to know the Poles and to entertain themselves. They have a big choice: several dozen theaters, including some really good ones, an impressive number of museums and art galleries, all types of academies, scientific centers, libraries. Good restaurants of all national cuisines, fashionable pubs and cafes in the Parisian type. Those who like the night life can play the roulette or lose money at night clubs and cabarets.

Płock is another interesting town in Mazovia. Its location is very picturesque on the high bank of the Vistula river. It is a very old town and once it used to be the most important one in this region. For some time it even played the role of Polish capital. A Romanesque cathedral on Wzgórze Tumskie is its pearl. Even today the inhabitants of Płock emphasize that they live in the Polish capital of the petrochemical industry, if of nothing else, because the biggest oil processing enterprise is located in the city.

Mazovia and Podlasie are highly similar in landscape. Podlasie has preserved much of its old glamour and natural character. Białystok is the capital of this region. It boasts a Baroque palace of the Braniecki family. Near Bielsko Podlaskie and Hajnówka there live several thousand Byelorussians. Most of them are Orthodox, but there are also some belonging to small religious sects of peculiar customs. An ethnographic attraction are the two villages of Bohoniki and Kruszyniany inhabited by Moslem Tartars for three centuries. A big horse stud is to be found in Janów Podlaski. Splendid Arab horses known all over the world are bred there.

Podlasie is also famous for two priceless treasures of virgin nature which are very rare in Europe. The valley of the slow-winding and clean Biebrza river has recently become a preserve which should make it better known. It is full of swamps and peatbogs, a real paradise for majestic elks and workaholic beavers, as well as numerous birds. There are rare species of wood and black grouse, and overwhelming numbers of water fowls. At winter's end when the snow melts and when rains fall, it is simply inaccessible to men. It can be crossed only by boats along a tangle of canals and small rivers.

The Białowieża Forest is much better known. It is the best preserved complex of natural lowland forests in Europe. The forest covers almost 1400 square kilometers (part of it is in Byelarus), out of which about 47 square kilometers constitute a strict natural reserve called Białowieski National Park. A walk through the backwoods is not an easy walk, it is a trip into the unknown and for careless tourists it may even turn out to be dangerous. It is easy to get lost or find oneself trapped. Old, decayed trees sometimes fall unexpectedly. There are 990 species of plants and 11000 species of animals (including 8550 insects). There are 55 species of mammals, including dee, roe deer, wild boars, badgers, lynx, wolfs, martens and weasels. But tourists go there to see the aurochs, truly royal animals considering that Polish kings started to protect them a thousand years ago. There was a time after the First World War when the species faced extermination. Poland managed to collect the remaining aurochs together, including those from zoological gardens, and to reconstruct the herd in the period between the two world wars. Nowadays most of them live outside the strict reserve and are free to wander the wood. Some of them have been transferred to other forests.

The auroch is a totally Polish peculiarity. The same is with the auroch vodka (żubrówka), a greenish vodka with a special grass added to it. Aurochs like to eat this species of grass, while people prefer it in an alcoholic beverage.

Lake-land and Pomerania

Northern Poland, from the Oder up to the Niemen river (outside Polish borders) is the land of the lakes. Glaciers influenced the landscape of this region considerably. When the climate got warmer and glaciers melted, there remained not only lakes (more than one thousand of them!), but also morainic hills made of sand, gravel and loam transported here by glaciers from Scandinavia. Forests covered the hills. Many lakes are interconnected by small, winding rivers. It is probably the most beautiful region in Poland. And the most original one because nowhere else in Europe, except Scandinavia, are there similar landscapes.

The wide old valley of the Vistula river separates the region into the Western Pomeranian and the Eastern Mazurian districts. More lakes are located in the western part, but bigger lakes are in the Big Lake District. Śniardwy lake, the biggest in Poland (110 square kilometers), where according to sailors there is often a high and vicious wave; the long lakes of Tałta and Jagodne, Śniardwy and Niegocin interconnected lakes and the tourist center of the region, Giżycko. Another big lake, Mamry, is part of a group of six interconnected lakes. How many different landscapes! Lakes where the far bank is not visible or hardly visible on the horizon. Others with countless bays and islands. Long lakes, regular gullies with high banks, as well as small lakes lost in the woods and often surrounded with peatbogs and reeds, so they are almost invisible. Absolute quiet, loneliness, and enormous fish!

There is a multitude of fish as a matter of fact. In the deepest waters there live lavarets and whitefish from the Salmonidae family (they are best roasted), big pikes in the reeds, and tenchein muddy places. Eels are the most precious trophies. It is the most expensive one and it is caught both by professional fishermen and by poachers. The water and swamp fowl is abundant as well. Some species are protected in reservations, for example, cranes, black storks, gray herons, black grouse, eagles and cormorants. Almost one out of three restaurants bears their names... Proud swans approach tourist camps to beg for food.

Among bigger animals, there are many deer and roe deer, sometimes elks, while in Borecka Forest there is a small herd of aurochs, and beavers construct their lodges. One can also encounter tarpans bred in order to restitute the species. Wild boars are everywhere, while wolves have become a rarity.

When a thousand years ago the Polish state was taking shape, there lived between the Oder and Vistula in the north a Pomeranian tribe closely connected with the Polanie. To the east of the Vistula there lived numerous tribes of Prussians, close relatives of the Lithuanians and Latvians. The Prussians were exterminated or germanized by the conquerors of these lands, the Teutonic Knights. A similar fate was faced by the Jadzwings, also close relatives of the Lithuanians, who left only numerous names of lakes and rivers in the Suwałki region, the easternmost part of the Masurian Lake District. The region has a different landscape: less forests, smaller lakes (apart from the large and exceptionally beautiful Wigry), while the morainic hills are good for skiing practice! The Lithuanian national minority lives in Sejny and Puńsk, cultivating still its language and customs. Augustów was chosen by several villages of Russian settlers who came there in the 17th century. They are old believers who did not accept the Orthodox Church and who protect their distinct beliefs and customs.

The Pomeranians grew either into the German or Polish nation. A small group, called the Słowińce, disappeared in the 20th century. Their neighbors, the Kashubs, had more luck. They lived in the middle part of Pomerania, which before the partitions belonged to Poland and was returned to it just after the First World War. Thus the Kashubs are ardent patriots, and preserve their own dialect which most Poles find difficult to understand.

The Masurians have a different history. They were Poles who settled in the land of the former Prussians, conquered politically by the Germans, many centuries ago. They adopted Protestantism, but spoke Polish and the majority of them considered themselves to be Poles while remaining under Germans rule. When after the Second World War Masuria was incorporated into Poland for the first time, the Masurians were subject to strict repressions on the part of the communist authorities and most of them emigrated to Germany. Only a few remained.

Olsztyn is the capital of the Masurian Lake District, although is it located in a historically different region, called Warmia, which, being an episcopal seat, had closer and earlier relations with Poland.

Two other cities situated at the borders of the Masurian Lake District are more interesting. Malbork on the Nogat river, one of the branches in the Vistula's delta, used to be the capital of the Teutonic Knights. A huge stronghold with few models in Europe was constructed in the Middle Ages. It is a complex of three castles, the oldest castle of which was erected at the beginning of the 13th century and surrounded with two rings of huge protective walls. In spite of numerous reconstructions, it continued in the Gothic style.

Toruń is located on the Vistula river. It is together with Cracow (or some people claim that even more than Cracow!) the most precious Polish city. The Gothic style predominates. Splendid medieval churches and significant fragments of municipal fortifications have been preserved. A Gothic town hall, made in the 13th and 14th centuries was reconstructed in the Mannerist style by the famous Flemish architect van Opbergen. Some buildings have Baroque facades. The great astronomer, who stopped the Sun and moved the Earth, Nicolaus Copernicus, was born there. It is a real pride of Toruń, which is also famous for baking wonderful, artistically adorned gingerbread.

The Lake District is directly connected with the Baltic seashore. For the first time in history, Poland has an access to the sea about half a thousand kilometers long.

The Baltic sea is not azure blue – it is gray. Its landscapes cannot be compared to those on the Riviera, Costa del Sol or the Adriatic Sea. Nevertheless, there is no lack of connoisseurs who prefer the Baltic pastel colors, buff dunes, pines leaning from frequent strong winds. In cloudy weather the northern cold is to be felt in the air. One who prefers Brueghel to Gauguin, chooses the Baltic sea.

The Poles are very sentimental about the sea because they had to fight for many centuries to have an access to it. Unfortunately, nobody remembers that Wolin, which is a small fishing settlement nowadays, and which was described in the 10th century by Ibrahim-ibn-Jacob, is older than the Polish state. It used to be a town with 12 gates in the walls and 300 ships in the port. Archeologists discovered Persian and Egyptian coins indicating widespread commercial relations.

Wolin is situated on an island of the same name. Its major part is constituted by a National Park with very interesting fauna. The most famous seaside resorts Międzyzdroje and Uznam are located in the Polish part on Uznam island. Świnoujście is also a roadstead of Szczecin which big ships cannot enter because it is 60 kilometres away from the sea at the mouth of the Oder river. Szczecin is a very old port town, which in the 11th century took over from Wolin. The inhabitants opposed Christianization for a long time, worshipping a three-headed god. Bolesław the Wrymouth managed to christianize the inhabitants of Szczecin at the beginning of the 12th century, although he must have achieved it not only by persuasion.

Szczecin had a very stormy history. It was conquered by the Dutch and by Brandenburg, by Swedes and Prussians, during the Napoleonic wars by the French and Russians. It was destroyed many times and inherited rather few monuments. Its present town layout in a radiate form of city squares and main streets, was designed in the 19th century on the basis of Haussmann's ideas; ths would explain Szczecin's resemblance of Paris, which was reconstructed by Haussmann.

In 1992 a new town appeared on the map of Poland: Borne Sulinowo. In truth, it has existed for several dozen years already, but being a secret town it was not marked on any map! Before the Second World War, a unit of the Wehrmacht stationed there, and afterwards the Red Army. Similar places, especially in Western Pomerania, Koszalin, Szczecin and Piła voivodships, were quite numerous. Training grounds were also secret and unaccessible to civilians, on lakes and in forests where nobody dared look for mushrooms... After the dissolution of the Warsaw Pact, the foreign army, which ceased to be Soviet and became Russian, left the territory of Poland and it turned out that our country had a few more beautiful regions to see.

Let us return to the sea. There is a chain of resorts, like beads on a neverending ribbon of sandy beeches. Nowhere on the Polish seashore is there a piece of a rocky shore like it is in the case of the Mediterranean Sea. Just sand and sand. If the weather is good in summer, milions of Polish and foreign visitors have the pleasure of seabathing and basking in the sun. Kołobrzeg, Ustka and Łeba are the most famous sea resorts. Their chief attraction are the high, shifting sand dunes, as if a miniature Sahara.

Poles, however, prefer the Hel peninsula, a peculiar shape of a scythe. It is 35 kilometers long, and about 1–2 kilometers wide (in some places merely several hundred meters). It is frequently threatened with being cut off from the mainland and returning to its state of many centuries ago when it was a chain of sandy shoals. In the old fishering town of Hel and places called Kuźnice and Jastarnia there live several hundred fishermen who go out to sea in small fishing boats and who are organized in old-fashioned cooperatives which also serve as clubs. This tradition is disappearing rapidly, however. Most Kashubs live of tourists who prefer to meet at Jurata, the most popular resort since the 1930s.

The Vistula Sandbar, similar to Hel, is located in the eastern part of the Polish seashore, but its end belongs to Russia. It separates the Baltic sea from the polluted Vistula Lagoon that directly neighbors with Żuławy, a fertile land around the mouth of the Vistula river. Once it was inhabited by Dutch settlers, who started to construct a system of channels, dams, flood gates and plodders torn from the sea and often situated in depressions.

There is an agglomeration called Trójmiasto in between the two peninsulas, on the Gdańska Bay. It is the most important city of the Polish coast.

Gdynia is the youngest part of it. Here, in a small fishing village newly independent Poland constructed its window out on the world – a big seaport. Construction commenced in the mid-1920s and before the Second World War Gdynia was already one of the busiest and most modern ports in the Baltic. It is still a prosperous, lively, well designed and beautiful city.

Sopot is situated farther to the east. Once it used to be a health resort with a famous casino. Its entertainment character has been preserved. The pier in Sopot is a promenade where it is proper to be seen in summer.

Still farther to the east is the third, biggest and best known city: Gdańsk.

It has always been a haughty and proud city. Conquered by the Teutonic Knights, it was always in opposition to them and intrigued always in Poland's favour.

In the end of the 15th century, Gdańsk returned to Poland but preserved its autonomy; kings had to reach agreements with the rich patricians. It was one of the wealthiest cities in Europe in the 16th and 17th centuries. It could afford to invite eminent artists who introduced the Flemish school and Italian Renaissance into Gothic art creating their own style, the so-called Gdańsk style.

After the first partition of Poland, in 1772, all of Pomerania came under Prussia's authority. Although Gdańsk was separated from Poland, it remained a Polish supporter. In the 19th century, it was germanized but not totally. After the First World War, it became a Free City, and a small Polish minority managed to maintain some influence, while the port region called Westerplatte remained under Polish authority.

The first shots of the Second World War were fired there on September 1, 1939, at 4.45 a.m. A small Polish garrison of less than two hundred people opposed the twenty times more numerous German forces for seven days.

Gdańsk was severely damaged during the war, but was quickly reconstructed. And again it showed its real character. In December 1970 historic workers' demonstrations against the communist authorities took place. They were suppressed. A young worker was among the rioters. His name was Lech Wałęsa. Ten years later he again led the workers from the Gdańsk shipyard. This was when the Solidarity union came into being. Again in vain, because a year and a half later the communists imposed martial law. Eight years later the Gdańsk shipyard again went on strike. The sequence of events which was initiated led to the abolition of communism in Poland, then in other European countries, and finally in the USSR itself. The first sparks of the flame of freedom were struck in Gdańsk. History will never forget it.

1. The Tatra. Panorama ▷

2. The Tatra. Rysy Group ▷

3. The Tatra. Morskie Oko
   and Czarny Staw lakes ▷

Carpathians and Subcarpathians

A panoramic view of the Tatra Mts. gives an idea of the variety of rock shapes, the steep slopes and craggy peaks rising majestically over the surrounding countryside [1]. The highest, most precipitous and rocky parts are the mostly granite Eastern Tatra, also known as the High Tatra, with their magnificent valleys and mountain meadows, towering peaks and mighty mountain massifs. At the foot of the precipitous, perpendicular or almost perpendicular rock faces there are piles of scree, and in the gullies, broken rock material.

In the main Tatra ridge there is the Rysy group of peaks [2]. The Slovak--Polish frontier, which runs along this ridge, deflects here sharply to the north towards Podhale. Of the three Rysy peaks, the highest one (2,503 m) is on the Slovak side of the frontier, the next highest (2,499 m) is on the boundary line and it is the highest peak of the Polish Tatra. The view from this peak is considered to be the most beautiful in the Tatra. On a fine day one can see all the most important peaks and mountain ridges, the Tatra valleys and lakes, and intermontane basins.

The largest and most beautiful mountain lake in Poland (covering an area of 34.5 ha) is Morskie Oko (Eye of the Sea) at an altitude of 1,393 m [3]. The name of the lake is derived from an old legend telling of its underground link with the sea. The highlanders also call it "The Lake of the Fish" because its crystal clear waters are the habitat of trouts. Dwarf mountain pines grow on the shores of the lake and clumps of spruce, rowan trees and also mountain stone pines. Czarny Staw (Black Lake), the second largest lake in the Tatra with area of 20.5 ha, is 191 m higher up. The stream which flows from it runs into Morskie Oko in a series of small waterfalls. Since the beginning of the 19th century these two lakes have been the main tourist attraction of the Tatra. (I.J.K.)

The Strążyska Valley (Dolina Strążyska) [4], formed by the mountain stream Strążyski, with its numerous cascades and the Siklawica Waterfall, is one of the most beautiful valleys in the Western Tatra. A trail to Mt. Giewont (1,909 m) leads through the valley. The rock face of Mt. Giewont rises 600 m above the upper parts of the Strążyska Valley. A deep cleft in the ridge of Mt. Giewont makes it look like the profile of a recumbent man. This has given rise to a legend about a sleeping knight.

The Chochołów Valley (Dolina Chochołowska) [5] is the westernmost valley in the Polish Tatra and also one of the largest and longest. It has numerous smaller valleys branching from it and in two places it narrows sharply forming what looks like rocky gateways. At one time iron ore was excavated in the valley. In the upper part of the valley, in the Chochołów Dale, there is a big tourist hostel; the shepherds' huts found there are vestiges of the once extensive sheep and cattle grazing. The dale is famous for the crocuses that bloom there in the spring. In the winter, the Chochołów valley is an attractive skiing area. (I.J.K.)

The Tatra form a natural habitat for high mountain flora found in similar climatic conditions in other mountain chains or in the far north. There are species here which occur in the Arctic as well as in the Central European and Eurasian mountain ranges. Ancient species from past geological epochs have also survived. The Tatra flora varies in accordance with altitude. On the lower level (950–1,250 m above sea level), spruce trees predominate with grey alders growing along streams and brooks. From 1,250 to 1,550 m, a dark, spruce forest takes over completely. At the forest's alpine limit there abound stone pines and European larch, both rare in Poland. Between 1,550 and 1,800 m dwarf mountain pines predominate, growing relatively densely at lower levels and breaking up into clumps and patches further up. Beyond the level of these mountain pines there there are no more trees. Strong winds, extreme variations in temperature and a shorter growing season restrict the flora to groundling vegetation resistant to the harsh climat. At the alpine level (1,800–2,300 m) the plant life alters in character, consisting largely of species and often subspecies specifically adapted to the mountains. The substratum greatly influences the plants existing here. The unique Tatra range exceeds 2,300 m in altitude; a series of rocky peaks and crags accommodates only very sparse mountain vegetation. Most alpine plants are protected as rare species.

Certain Tatra plant species grow in relation to the substratum. The richest varieties are associated with a limestone base; sandstone is less fertile and a granite substratum even less fertile in terms of the variety of species. Gentians, dwarf and glacial buttercups, small primroses, alpine campanula, spotted gentians and leopards's banes are found exclusively on the granite substratum of the Upper Tatra [15].

Alpine violets, octopetalous mountain avens [8], alpine buttercup, spring gentian, alpine edelweiss [9], mountain aster, Tatra saxifrage and mountain primrose [11] grow on the considerably more fertile limestone base.

A number of these plant species exist only in the alpine meadows above the treeline; for instance, the octopetalous mountain aven [8], the Gentiana frigida [10], Salix veticulata, Silene acaulis, Gentiana Clusii [15, 16], the alpine violet and the montain primrose [11]. Others grow mainly on screes, i.e. the alpine poppy [13] and dwarf buttercup, in rock crevices, like the mountain primrose [11], or in damper gullies and in places where the snow lies longer, for instance the alpine buttercup or Tatra saxifrage. Aconites, Tatra larkspur [17, Mulgedium alpinum, Ademostyles alliana and spotted gentian form a rich

4. The Tatra. Strążyska valley

5. The Tatra. Chochołowska valley

6. The Tatra. Cable car line

7. Zakopane. „Pod Jedlami" villa

30

association of herbs at the borderline between the alpine meadows and the dwarf mountain pine levels.

The Upper Tatra peaks are characterised by ground plants such as lichens and liverworts as well as a small number of grasses and herbs like Gentiana frigida [10] which tolerate harsh environments. This vegetation grows in unevenly dispersed clumps in places where thin pockets of clay have collected between fells and crags.

Alpine edelweiss [15] and carlines [19] are often used motifs in regional folk art, being the most common and popular species found in the Tatra, although the latter plant also grows as far away as in the Polish Uplands. (I.J.K.)

The Tatra fauna is also characterised by alpine species, such as the chamois [19] and marmot, which have been under protection since 1868. Bears, lynxes and ermines are rare sights these days, stags and roe deer, badgers, polecats, weasels, martens and in some parts even wild boars are somewhat more common. The rarest and perhaps most highly prized of the area's birdlife is the golden eagle, although no less typical and also threatened with extinction are the wallcreepers, sparrow hawks, mountain wagtails, water pipets and water ouzels. Among the lizards, the spotted salamander [18] is particularly noteworthy for its exquisitely coloured skin. A species of brianchial shellfish is a diluvial survivor confined to two small neighbouring lakes in the High Tatra known as the Double Pond. Insect life is modest in variety but also highly specific. Legal protection and human care facilitates the preservation of rare species threatened with extinction.

Mount Kasprowy Wierch (1,985 m) in the main Tatra ridge constitutes a border peak in the Western Tatra. It rises above a series of beautiful valleys: Goryczkowa, Kasprowa, Gąsienicowa and Cicha. From Kasprowy Wierch, visited by many tourists, there is a panoramic view of the surrounding peaks and valleys comprising the High and Western Tatra ranges. An astronomical observatory in the vicinity has the highest location in Poland. Of the many excellent ski runs operating during the winter months, the best known descends steeply down Kasprowy Wierch, through the nearby meadows of Hala Gąsienicowa and forests as far as Zakopane. Kasprowy Wierch, lying at the heart of numerous tourist trails and offering wonderful vistas, is a popular attraction. A cable car line [6] opened in 1934, beginning at the Kuźnice district of Zakopane, makes this popular peak easily accessible.

Cable cars pass over the Bystra Valley forests to an interchange at Myślenickie Turnie from where the journey may be continued to the Kasprowy Wierch station. Mountain climbing and hiking as well as skiing attract many visitors. Tourism in the Tatra boasts a long tradition. Stanisław Staszic, a major figure of the late Polish Enlightenment who conducted research in the Tatra between 1803 and 1805, is regarded as the inspirer of "taternictwo", the

8–17. Tatra flora

Polish counterpart of alpinism. Zako- pane region highlanders, who during the 19th century frequently accompa- nied visitors through the mountains, finally set up their own professional guide group. Today they dominate the Mountain Rescue (GOPR) responsible for tourist safety. During the Nazi occupation, mountain guides served as cross-border couriers for the Polish resistance movement. (I.J.K.)

Zakopane, the so-called winter capital of Poland [20], is situated at the foot of the northern slopes of the Tatra between Giewont and Gubałówka peaks. It is the largest tourist and winter-sports centre in Poland. There are many tourist trails and ski lifts, as well as a cable car link to Kasprowy Wierch. Ski jumps allow co- mpetitions, also of international status, to be organized. Hot springs in Jasz- czurówka have enabled Zakopane to develop as a health resort. The town is situated at an altitude of 800–1,000 m. It started as a mountain village in the 16th century. An iron foundry operated in Kuźnica, the highest part of Zakopane, in the 17th century. It was still func- tioning in the 19th century. By this time the town was already beginning to ex- pand as a centre for people visiting the mountains. The first recorded moun- taineering expeditions date back to the late 18th century and the first hostel was built in 1823. The development of Zako- pane as a tourist centre began in earnest during the 19th century. Dr. Tytus Cha- łubiński popularised the climatic values and beautiful scenery of the Tatra mountain in his writings, and the much celebrated Tatra Club was founded in 1873. The number of visitors as well as holiday makers and people seeking to repair their health increased tenfold. The tourist trade expanded, especially once the town was connected by rail with Cracow in 1899. Zakopane also became a favourite haunt of the intellec- tual and artistic elites of Cracow and Warsaw. Between the world wars people from all over Poland visited it in num- bers. Municipal status was granted in 1933. During the 1939–1945 war Zako- pane was closed to Polish tourists and was exploited as a resort for Nazi sol- diers and dignitaries. At the same time it also became a centre for the Polish resistance movement which dispatched many people across the border from here. Today the Tatra tourist trade is estimated to attract several million peo- ple annually, most of whom stay in Zakopane itself. The number of visitors vastly exceeds that of permanent resi- dents. The main street, Krupówki, whe- re social life and commerce are concent- rated, has become a busy street typical of much larger cities. Many sports events and artistic meetings are held here, and several are connected with the local folklore of which Zakopane rema- ins a major centre. (I.J.K.)

As Zakopane developed, the building style changed. Alongside the old timber houses and farmsteads of the highland- ers, villas were built which kept to the

18,19. Tatra fauna

traditional highland style, for instance, the "Pod Jedlami" Villa [7] which was designed by Stanisław Witkiewicz, the author of the Zakopane style. Modern buildings, especially those constructed in the last thirty years, have increasingly departed from the old style.

In Zakopane there are many sanatoria, holiday centres, tourist hostels and hotels. Examples of the original highland architecture and art have been preserved there. It also has some interesting museums. Valuable ethnographic and geological collections and examples of the flora and fauna of the Tatra can be seen in the Tatra Museum founded in 1888. In 1972, the Karol Szymanowski Museum was opened in "Villa Atma", where the composer lived and worked. It was there that he composed *Harnasie*, a ballet based on highland motifs. (I.J.K.)

For centuries shepherds have used the high alpine meadows of the Tatra, which in Polish are called "hale", for seasonal grazing [21]. In spring, under the supervision of flock masters known as "baca", shepherd boys – "juhas" in Polish – used to drive the flocks of sheep belonging to their villages high up into the mountains. They lived in wooden huts and were helped in their work by white Podhale sheepdogs. In their mountain shelters, the shepherds would process ewes' milk into cheeses called "bunc", "bryndza" and "oscypki". The shepherds had their own customs and special utensils for collecting the milk and turning it into cheese. This was the main occupation of highlanders inhabiting the extensive Podhale Basin. Today they are largely engaged in farming. Pastures have been greatly reduced since grazing was prohibited in the Tatra National Park. The spring and autumn "redyk", i.e. driving of the sheep up to the mountain pastures and bringing them back down before the cold set in, still takes place, although in changed form. Today the sheep are taken by train to the Low Beskids, the Bieszczady and Sudeten Mountains.

The villages of Podhale have retained their rich, lively and picturesque mountain folklore. The region was settled in the Middle Ages by people moving in from the Cracow area, German colonists and later by Wallachian shepherds. Hungarian and Slovakian influences as well as those of passing Gypsies were greatly felt as well. The folklore arising from this ethnic mixture is consequently rich and unique, reflected particularly in the colourful costumes [22] worn till the present day, especially on religious occasions and during local festivals. Men wear trousers of thick white, woollen cloth embroidered with a characteristic motif ("parzenica"), sleeveless sheepskin waistcoats ("serdak") and round hats decorated with small shells. Younger highland women embroider their laced waistcoats with flower motifs inspired by the local flora and wear them over richly designed linen blouses and flower-patterned skirts. See them whir-

20. Zakopane. View from Mt. Gubałówka

21. Podhale ▷

ling round and round in the rapid highland robbers dance called the "zbójnicki". (I.J.K.)

To a greater extent than most of Poland's mountain regions, the Podhale has managed to keep alive its traditional folk arts and crafts. Wood has served both in architecture (churches, cottages) and sculpture (roadside shrines, altar figures). Similar methods and styles are manifested on both sides of the Carpathians, as much on the Slovak as the Polish side. A highlander's house can be identified by its harmonious plan and perfect proportions, the attractive natural colour of its wooden walls and its shingle roof. Several such houses have been preserved in the village of Chochołów [23] to the west of Zakopane.

The most sublime achievements of highland carpentry are reflected in the exceptional beauty of the rural church architecture. High shingle roofs with signatures and shingle turrets resemble Gothic brick architecture with its defensive character and large spaces. The church in Dębno is one of the oldest wooden churches in this region [24]. It was erected in the second half of the 15th century and is famous for its ornate carpentry and the well preserved polychromy from the turn of the 15th century, consisting of geometrical, floral, architectural, animal and figural motifs, includings St. George and the dragon. The main altar contains a painted triptych from the early 16th century, typical of the decorative arts of Małopolska at the time. The original wooden tabernacle with Gothic motifs comes from the same period. The oldest known surviving panel painting in Poland was discovered at Dębno; it is part of a 13th century altar representing two saints. The interiors are additionally decorated with sculptures designed by a contemporary local craftsman. Altogether, the unusually rich and colourful combination of folkloristic and professional art lends a truly remarkable atmosphere to this small interior. (P.T.)

The Pieniny, a small rugged limestone mountain chain, is famed for its wonderful scenery and luxuriant vegetation. The entrance to the Pieniny Mts. is guarded by two castles: Czorsztyn and Niedzica, former border strongholds along the trade route from Poland to Hungary and also the meeting place of diplomats from both countries. The 13th century Czorsztyn castle was enlarged by Casimir the Great in the 14th century. At the end of the 18th century it was destroyed by fire and was never rebuilt. The Niedzica castle [28], on the right bank of the River Dunajec, was built by Hungarian magnates in the 14th century. Hungarian and Polish noblemen passed it back and forth between themselves, and in the 16th century it was for a time the seat of outlaw robber knights. In 1945 it came into the possession of the Polish State. It consisted of the upper Gothic castle which is in ruins today and the lower castle rebuilt in the Renaissance style. The lower castle today houses a retreat for art historians.

22. Podhale. Traditional highlander costumes

23. Podhale. Chochołów

24. Dębno. Church

25. Dębno. Church interior

27. Pieniny. Dunajec Gorge

◁ 26. Pieniny. Trzy Korony peak

The vegetation of the Pieniny Mts. is very luxuriant. The slopes are covered with fir and beech forests with some larch and yew trees. The mountain meadows are filled with grass and flowers. On the warmer limestone rocks there are still relics of Tertiary vegetation represented by the aromatic Zawadzki chrysanthemum. The highest and most varied part of the Pieniny Mts. is the Trzy Korony (Three Crowns) massif [26], the main peak of which is Okrąglica (982 m), a magnificent viewpoint overlooking the Dunajec Gorge. The river crosses the Pieniny in a narrow and deep valley [27]. It forms a deep bend with seven meanders 9 km long. The Dunajec Gorge is considered to be one of the most beautiful in Europe and one of the tourist attractions there is floating the rapids on rafts made of dugouts bound together.

The river is also known for its sudden rises in water level which cause flooding. In order to regulate its flow (and also to provide electricity), dams and reservoirs have been built in Rożnów and Czchów. A dam and reservoir is also currently being constructed in Czorsztyn, under heavy fire from environment and landscape protection groups.

The Pieniny National Park was founded in 1954 to protect the beautiful natural landscape of the Pieniny Mts. It is regarded as one of Poland's most attractive tourist spots owing to the varied landscape, rugged crags, the beautiful Dunajec Gorge and the meadows which abound in flowers. (I.J.K.)

North of the Pieniny lie the Beskids. To the southwest, the boundary peak is Wielka Racza (1,236 m) belonging to a mountain group which is part of the Żywiec Beskids [29]. In the forests of the Wielka Racza there are beautiful, large clearings which are excellent skiing areas [30]. The ski run down the western slope of the mountain to the Slovak side is regarded as one of the best in the Beskids.

The most westerly part of the Beskids, the Silesian Beskids, consists of the Czantoria Chain and the Barania Góra group. The Czantoria Chain is lower and the slopes are gentler. Czantoria Wielka is the highest peak (995 m). In the Barania Góra group, the main peak Skrzyczne rises to an altitude of 1,257 m, and Barania Góra itself is 1,220 m high. It is on the slopes of Barania Góra that the two sources of the Vistula, Biała and Czarna Wisełka, spring. The Barania Góra group is a very popular tourist and recreation area, visited in particular by the inhabitants of the nearby Upper Silesian industrial district. The most well known resorts include Wisła, Brenna, Bystra, Szczyrk, Jaszowiec and Ustroń.

In the depression between the Silesian Beskids and the Żywiec Beskids there is a village called Koniaków, which is

28. Pieniny. Niedzica castle

29. Silesian Beskids. View from Pilsko towards Wielka Racza ▷

famed for the lace made there [31]. The women of another village, Istebna, have also mastered this rare craft in Poland. In both of these villages one can see people in regional costumes any day. In many places in the Beskids highland folklore is easily recognized in the unique architecture, carvings, paintings, music, dances and colourful folk costumes. (I.J.K.)

Wadowice is a town located at the foot of the Small Beskids on the River Skawa, a tributary of the Vistula, at the junction of several railway lines and roads. It has also been an industrial centre since the 19th century.
In the 16th century Wadowice was known for a town school run by the burghers. It became famous in 1978 when Karol Wojtyła, born and brought up in Wadowice, became Pope John Paul II. The Pope's birth and christening are registered in the local parish church, rebuilt in the Baroque style during the 18th century. The Wojtyła family flat has been adapted to serve as a museum dedicated to the Pope.
Kalwaria Zebrzydowska, situated between the Makowski Beskids and Wieliczka Plateau, was created in 1617 by the Cracow voivode Mikołaj Zebrzydowski as a pilgrim settlement attached to a Bernardine monastery founded in 1602. It has continued to carry out this function to the present day. The originally mannerist monastery buildings raised from 1603 to 1609 were later rebuilt in the baroque style [34], and were surrounded to the north and east by 42 predominantly mannerist calvary chapels erected on hillocks and in valleys from the early 17th into the 19th century. A mystery play originating from the 18th century, known as the *Way of the Cross*, is performed annually during the Holy Week preceding Easter by peasant actors from neighbouring villages. (I.J.K.)

A historic urban layout and a characteristic group of wooden town buildings of the 19th century can be seen in Lanckorona. Around the market square and along several streets there are picturesque single – storey buildings with projecting eaves and high shingle roofs. The highest mountains belonging to the Beskids are in the Babia Góra group [35]. This is an asymmetrical range with steep northern faces which are rocky in places and crossed by numerous valleys and springs, and southern, gently descending slopes. The highest peak, Mt.Babia Góra (1725 m) has a rocky summit called "Diablak" covered with broken rock debris. The slopes of Babia Góra are richly forested up to an altitude of 1400 m below which (up to 1150 m) there grow fir and beech trees.

30. Silesian Beskids. View from Pilsko towards the Tatra

31. Silesian Beskids. Lace producers from Koniaków

32. Silesian Beskids. Biała Wisełka

Higher up stretch dwarf mountain pines opening out onto flowering alpine meadows. The Babia Góra National Park was set up to protect this natural landscape. (I.J.K.)

The Wiśnicz Castle [37] located on a wooded prominence over the Leksandrówka river valley was built before 1500 by a powerful local family. In the first half of the 15th century the last of the family, Piotr III Kmita, changed it into a residence. The Kmita family then sold the castle to the Lubomirski magnates at the end of the 16th century. The Cracow voivode Stanisław Lubomirski founded the town of Wiśnicz Nowy in 1616 and set up the Carmelite church and monastery on a hill facing the castle. The castle was rebuilt between 1615 and 1621. At that time the Italian architect Matteo Trapola was responsible for designing all the Lubomirskis' buildings. His evident vacillation between the mannerist tradition and modern baroque found an interesting expression in the entrance gate. The castle and monastery were surrounded with typical Italian fortifications including pentagonal bastions. The loggia located in the castle's small inner courtyard, the chapel and extended residential building, including a main hall supported on two pillars, were most likely designed by the same architect. Stanisław Lubomirski was a collector and patron of the arts. Some of the earliest performances of Italian opera in Poland were staged at Wiśnicz. In the 17th century, the Swedish army carried away nearly fifty cartloads of valuable furniture, tapestries and paintings. The castle was inhabited until 1780 and underwent extensive restoration in 1909, 1928 and during the late 1980s. The interiors have retained little to attest to the castle's former glory; parts of the original stucco designed by J.C.Falconi have survived as well as fragments of polychromy in the chapel, early baroque fireplaces and portals in the early baroque style. (P.T.)

Lipnica Murowana, located on a busy trail to Hungary, used to be a rich town in the Middle Ages. Three churches are proof of past prosperity. St. Leonard's Church [38], constructed in the second half of the 15th century, is one of the oldest wooden churches in Poland.
The nave of the church is surrounded with open arcades ("soboty") designed to protect congregations in bad weather. Polychromy covers the interiors. Three late Gothic triptychs have been preserved till the present day. (P.T.)

34. Kalwaria Zebrzydowska. Bernardine monastery complex

35. High Beskids. Babia Góra

33. Wadowice. House where Pope John-Paul II was born.

Nowy Sącz [41], lying at the confluence of the Kamienica and Dunajec rivers, is the capital of the Sącz region. It arose as a royal frontier town founded in 1292 by Vaclav II, king of Bohemia and Poland. A castle was raised and the town was encircled with defensive walls during the reign of Casimir the Great in the 14th century. The trade with Hungary brought prosperity and as a royal town Nowy Sącz was granted many privileges. The crafts and arts flourished. A parish school opened in the early 15th century. Jan Długosz, 15th century historian, diplomat, royal canon and personal tutor to the sons of King Casimir Jagiellon wrote his history of Poland while staying in Nowy Sącz. Here Michał Sędziwój (Sendivogius Polonus), a renowned alchemist wrote an alchemist treatise which was later translated into many languages and reprinted more than fifty times between 1604 and 1797. The goden age in Nowy Sącz's economic and cultural history ended with the first Swedish invasion of Poland in the mid 17th century. Military operations, looting by the invading armies, fires and epidemics caused widespread destruction and loss of life. A rebellion against the Swedes broke out in 1655 and Nowy Sącz was among the first Polish towns to be freed. Never to regain its former status, the town experienced prolonged economic stagnation. In the 19th century a new era of urban expansion dawned with the opening of a railway line, when food processing, chemical and wood industries began to develop. A large railroad repair works was opened in 1900. The town was an important centre for the Polish resistance during the last war, and one third of its population was exterminated by the Nazis. In January 1945 it was spared total destruction when stores of explosives in the castle where the Nazis were stationed were blown up. Despite the numerous calamities in its past, Nowy Sącz can still boast many historic monuments, including some dating back to the Middle Ages.

Straddling the Poprad and Dunajec rivers, Stary Sącz [40] traces its origins back to the 10th century. Like Nowy Sącz, it belonged to the system of fortified towns guarding the "Hungarian" route and prospering from the associated trading; it suffered a similar fate in the 17th century when the Swedish invasion arrested its development. The oldest religious school for women was set up here in the Clarist nunnery. Łącko, on the fringes of an extensive fruit-growing area, is also an historic town. The apple orchards in this part of the Sącz region number some 50,000 trees. The "Blooming Apple Tree" holiday is organized every May in Łącko. The plum brandy from Łącko is widely acclaimed.

37. Wiśnicz Nowy. Castle

38. Lipnica Murowana.
St. Leonard's Church ▷

To the south of Stary Sącz there are the Sącz Beskid mountains which are divided into two ranges, the Radziejowa and Jaworzyna, by the charming Poprad valley. Alpine meadows stretching below the high peaks contain some interesting rock formations.

There are many health resorts and spas in the Sącz Beskids, famed for their mineral waters. Żegiestów is picturesquely situated on the southern slopes of the Poprad valley; Muszyna and Piwniczna are also on the Poprad. Szczawnica in the picturesque Grajcarek valley between the Pieniny mountains and Sądecki Beskids developed from a Carpathian village into a well known spa in the second half of the 19th century. The most popular resort and largest spa in the Beskids is Krynica, known as "the pearl of Polish spas". Mineral springs abound, including the Zubr Spring which is one of the most abundant acidulous-alkaline springs in Europe. The healing properties of Krynica's spring waters were discovered in the 18th century. The spa developed rapidly in the second half of the last century. Apart from the older timber architecture [39], modern sanatoria and holiday homes are becoming increasingly numerous. Krynica and the other regional spas also operate as tourist centres; the natural beauty of the Sącz Beskids makes them ideal for rest, hiking, skiing and enjoying the landscape. (I.J.K.)

The shepherds and farmers inhabiting until recently the Beskid foothills were Greek-Catholic and Orthodox Christians. They left behind them wooden religious temples, representing the greatest penetration to the west of the Orthodox culture. Their church architecture was greatly influenced by western monumentalism, reflected in the Gothic plan as well as the Baroque style of the belltower crowns and interior design. The liturgy, however, remained purely Orthodox, while the structural and technical aspects of the Gothic and Baroque styles were applied to wooden architecture. Religious temples in Powroźnik from 1643 [42], Wojkowa from 1790 and Dubne from 1863 [43] represent Greek Catholic churches designed by the local population, the Lemks. Graceful belltowers with overhanging tops, slate roofs and picturesque location among old trees represent common characteristics shared with Catholic churches of this region. The eastern orientation is emphasised by the clear tripartite division into the presbytery, aisles and belltower rising above the church portal. The Orthodox church interiors consist of a portal where women gathered ("babiniec"), aisles designed for men and the presbytery shielded from the nave by the iconostasis. Religious buildings and cottages of the Lemks were frequently painted on the

◁ 39. Krynica. Old wooden houses

◁ 40. Stary Sącz. Southwestern view

41. Nowy Sącz

42. Powroźnik. Orthodox church

outside, usually in one colour or a combination of deep red, navy blue and ochre. Unfortunately, little of the colours has remained. Rustic shingle roofs are increasingly being replaced with tin; consequently, the complex line of these structures is becoming overly simplified. This exceptionally interesting group of architectural monuments, which appeared at the junction of East and West is rapidly disappearing. (P.T.)

Biecz [44], one of the most charming and ancient towns of the Subcarpathians on the banks of the River Ropa, was at one time called "the little Cracow". In the 14th and 16th centuries Biecz also prospered from trade with Hungary; the late medieval tower is a remnant of the defence walls put up at that time. The town hall possesses a tower from the same period and a monumental parish church was constructed between 1516 and 1521. The church's late medieval interiors have retained many valuable works of art, including a painting from the school of Michelangelo and a sculptured Renaissance music stand.

Sanok prospered from trade with the Hungarian provinces as well. In 1958 a museum of local architecture for the eastern Subcarpathians was organised there [45], devoted above all to such ethnographic groups as the Lemks, Bojkos and Pogórzans. More than seventy wooden structures are located over an area of twenty six hectares: cottages, entire farm complexes and service buildings, Orthodox churches preserving their interiors, the oldest of which originate from the 18th century. The History Museum of Sanok houses the largest, most valuable collection of icon paintings in Poland, covering the period from the 14th to the 19th century.

The interiors of the mid-18th century church in Dukla [46] are attractive for their design so typical of the rococo. The burial chamber of Amelia Brühel Mniszech, who died in 1772, is particularly interesting. Its designer, more than likely Jan Obrocki, lent it the shape and visual impact of a palatial rococo boudoir. The deceased woman was made immortal, resting on a black marble plinth surrounded with great mirrors, caught in contemplation over a fashionable novel. The sculpture achieved spectacular effects in the way it presented the intricate folds and frills of the dress. This sculpture belongs to the renowned late-baroque Lvov school.

Another conspicuous example of wooden church architecture can be found in the village of Szalowa [47]; it is

44. Biecz

45. Sanok. Open-air folk museum

46. Dukla. Tomb of Amalia Mniszech in the church

47. Szalowa. Wooden church interiors

48. Bieszczady. View from Wietlińska Połonina ▷

a three-aisled church, erected in the years 1739–1756, whose originality lies in the architect's attempt to create a monumental, late-baroque edifice in wood. The interiors have a colourful decor from the mid-1700s which is uniform in character and succeeds in synthesising both baroque and rococo forms as well as folk traditions with the demands of professional art. (P.T.)

The unspoilt natural beauty of the Bieszczady, Poland's most peripheral mountain group, has begun to attract increasing numbers of visitors. The main bases for excursions are located in Ustrzyki Górne, Cisna and Komańcza, in the latter of which there is an interesting Greek-Catholic church built in 1805. Of all the Beskid ranges, only the Bieszczady lack the upper level forests; their uppermost parts are overgrown with tall grasses, abundant flowers and alder shrubs. These extensive alpine meadows, known as "połoniny", offer excellent views [48] and, in winter, good ski slopes. The best known "połoniny", Caryńska and Wetlińska [50], have been used for many years as summer grazing grounds. These areas have been partially incorporated into the Bieszczady National Park. The lower mountain levels are covered with beech forests or mixed fir and beech forests, growing no further than the exceptionally low altitude of 1200 m. The steep mountain slopes are broken up in places by mountain streams which feed the River San.

As a western branch of the Eastern Carpathians, the Bieszczady consist of long parallel mountain ridges divided by wide depressions. The highest peaks in the Polish part of the range are Mt. Tarnica (1346 m) and the neighbouring peaks of Krzemień and Halicz [49], both rising to a height of 1335 m. Wielka Rawka is somewhat lower (1304 m) but constitutes the main peak of the ridge forming the border between Poland, Ukraine and Slovakia.

Prior to the Second World War, the Bieszczady were quite densely populated and had a highly developed agriculture. During the fighting against the Ukrainian Nationalists in 1944 – 1947, most of the settlements were burned down and the population was largely resettled either in the Soviet Union or in various parts of the so-called Oder-Neisse territories handed over to the post-1944 Peoples' Republic of Poland. Solitary houses or Orthodox churches frequently are the only vestiges of the once many villages [52]. A resettlement and cultivation program was initiated in the 1950s but the Bieszczady still remain one of the most sparsely populated areas of Poland. The local population lives mainly of forestry and shepherding. Animals are

49. Bieszczady. Halicz

50. Bieszczady. Dales ▷

51. Bieszczady. Solina lake ▷

52. Bieszczady. Piątkowa.
Orthodox church ▷

transported from the Podhale and Western Beskids for summer grazing. The unique natural scenery and attractiveness of the pioneer conditions prevailing here, serve to draw increasing numbers of tourists. But man remains little more than a guest in the Bieszczady and rarely ventures deep into the wild country beyond the marked trails and tourist routes.

The animal life has remained to this day abundant; deers and wild boars are particularly common. European bisons have been introduced recently. Wolves, lynx and bears still hold their own, and among the birds the golden eagle. There are also venomous snakes in the area. The still abundant wildlife attracts hunters, particularly in winter. (I.J.K.)

The northern Bieszczady foothills are less densely forested and more densely populated. Lake Solina [51] attracts the most tourists. It was created in 1968 following the building of a dam and hydroelectric station on the River San above Lesko. Although in surface area (21 km²) this reservoir comes only sixth among Poland's artificial lakes, it is the deepest (82 m) and holds the greatest volume of water (506 milion m³). The surrounding scenery increases Lake Solina's appeal as a tourist attraction and place for water sports. Modern summer houses and camping sites have mushroomed. Solina and Polańczyk are the most popular local tourist centres. Towards Lesko there is a second dam at Myszyce, creating a smaller artificial lake of the same name which has also been developed as a rest and leisure centre. (I.J.K.)

When Marcin Krasicki, voivode of Podolia and a count of the Holy Roman Empire, became owner of Krasiczyn in 1598, he set about rebuilding the late-medieval castle into an extensive residence raised around a central, rectangular courtyard [53]. Italian architects designed the castle in the mannerist style, composed of symbolic elements. Krasicki obviously intended his residence to reflect and express the then recognised theoretical hierarchy of the world; the four corner bastions were named after the Holy Father ("Boska"), the Pope ("Papieska"), the Sovereign („Królewska") and the Gentry ("Szlachecka"). These names were reflected in the design of each of these bastions; for example, the "Holy Father Tower" was built as a chapel. The galleries of the interconnecting wings of Krasiczyn Castle are adorned with busts of the Holy Roman emperors, biblical scenes, portraits of Polish monarchs and figures of knights, lords and saints. Each wing received an attic of contrasting design and artistic programme.

The panorama of part of the Old Town in Przemyśl [54] fails to give a full impression of this beautifully situated and historic city on the San's steeply rising escarpment. The earliest record of Przemyśl comes from 981, although the city's most prized architectural treasures date to the 15th to 17th centuries when it experienced the acme of its development. Prized collections of icons and artistic tapestries from the period are housed in local museums. Przemyśl and Jarosław lay on a busy trade route between Ruthenia

53. Krasiczyn. Castle

54. Przemyśl. Old Town

55. Jarosław. Orsetti family townhouse

57. Łańcut. Palace

58. Łańcut. Palace interiors

56. Leżajsk. The Bernardine church organs

and Hungary. In the 16th and 17th centuries merchants built arcaded town houses following Italian models, of which the most splendid to come down to our own times actually belonged to an Italian merchant family, the Orsettis [55]. It was built in the Old Town Square in Jarosław and possessed a characteristic developed attic.

The magnificent organ in the Bernardine church of Leżajsk [56] was designed after 1678; it spans the three aisles. The themes of the organ's decoration refer to mankind's redemption under the Church's guidance with a representation of the Madonna, and the symbolic struggle between the Catholic Church and other religious denominations during the Counter Reformation depicted in the central scene of the confrontation between Hercules and the Hydra.

The early-Baroque palace at Łańcut [57] was built in the years 1629-1641 by the architect Matteo Trapola. Retaining the inner, square courtyard and four corner towers, the palace was altered and enlarged several times. Surrounded by stately park grounds, it presently houses a museum containing collections of painting, sculpture, porcelain, Gobelin tapestries and period furniture [58]. It is the spot of many cultural events. (P.T.)

The Baranów Castle near Sandomierz [59] was designed for the Leszczyński family in the years 1591–1606, probably in accordance with plans drawn up by the Florentine architect and sculptor, Santi Gucci. The castle represents a synthesis of an arcaded courtyard residence [60], of which Cracow's Wawel Castle constituted the model in Poland, and the mannerist style. Santi Gucci, who came to Poland in the mid-1500s, brought with him the sublimated forms of Florentine mannerism. Gucci took full advantage of his status as court artist and his rights to the stone quary in Pińczów, which the Polish monarch leased to him, in order to implement an ambitious building and sculptural program, continued by associates after his death in 1600.

The castle was built on a regular plan with corner towers lending it a false defensive character. The exterior facade with its high attic constitutes a mere screen enclosing the courtyard. Among the unexpected effects typical of mannerist design, the entrance gate does not operate as a carriage entrance, but conceals a staircase leading onto the richly adorned courtyard, where presently concerts and theatrical events are frequently held. The castle, restored with funds from the sulphur industry, is used as a museum in part. (P.T.)

Tarnów [61] was founded in the Middle Ages, but blossomed as an economic and cultural centre in the 15th and 16th centuries. The Gothic town hall [78] received late-Renaissance embellishments during rebuilding in the later part of the 16th century, its new attic being inspired by Cracow's Cloth Hall, in particular the mascarons. The Gothic cathedral dates from the 14th century and houses a remarkable tomb

59. Baranów Sandomierski. Castle

62. Wieliczka. Chapel of St. Kinga in the salt mine

60. Baranów Sandomierski. Castle courtyard

61. Tarnów

designed by the Italian sculptor, Giovanni Maria Mosca of Padua, known as Padovano, who worked in Poland after 1532. The tomb, originally designed in 1561–1567, contained the remains of hetman Jan Tarnowski, but was remodelled as a two-level tomb following the death in 1567 of the old commander's son Jan Krzysztof. It is an exquisite example of late-Renaissance sculpture, relating to Venetian models. As a whole, it is a representative of the two-level tombs with sleeping figures which became exceptionally popular in the 16th and early 17th century Poland, inspired by the Humanist achievements of the Italian Renaissance. The deceased are accompanied by personifications of the virtues Justice, Prudence, Victory and Glory. The Museum of the Diocese, operating since the late-19th century and located in a complex of medieval houses next to the cathedral, contains late-medieval collections of Małopolska paintings and sculpture surpassed in quality and value only by those displayed in Cracow. (P.T.)

The vilage of Zalipie near Dąbrowa Tarnowska is a well known centre of folk art. The traditional folk painting, which practically died out in the 19th century, was revived in Zalipie in the years between world wars. On the initiative of one of the village women, Felicja Curyłowa, all the village housewives began painting the quoins of their cottages and adorning the interiors with plant motifs. After Curyłowa's death (1974) a museum of folk art was arranged in her cottage [63]. (I.J.K.)

Wieliczka lies in between the Wieliczka and Bochnia foothills. As a settlement it sprung up to serve the salt mines. The salt seams shaped the town's evolution, a fact reflected in its first documented name, Wielka Sól (Magnum Sal). Salt mining in Wieliczka goes back to at least the 9th century. The mine's enlargement is associated with the name of Kinga, wife of the Cracow prince, Bolesław the Chaste (1226–1279). The mine, which belonged to the royal family, was leased to the magnates. Following Poland's partition in 1772, the mine passed into Austrian hands and since 1918 it has belonged to the Polish state. Even today salt is extracted in places, although the most ancient parts have been adapted as a museum, famous for its beautiful underground corridors and chambers, the more renowned of which include two chapels containing altars and sculptures named after St. Anthony and the Holy Cross, designed in the 17th century, and Blessed Kinga, from the 19th century [62]. Numerous statues have been carved out of the salt walls. The museum traces the mine's history and methods of both extracting and transporting the salt to the Middle Ages. Some chambers are used for medical purposes. The fabulous Crystal Grotto has been placed under strict protection. It was discovered during the exploitation of salt. The walls are cov-

63. Zalipie. Cottage interiors

ered with salt crystals about 10 cm long, but there are also some crystals up to 40 cm. The salt mines of Wieliczka are a unique monument on a world scale. (I.J.K.)

Oświęcim is situated almost in the centre of the Oświęcim Basin. As an important stronghold, it was marked on a map made by the Arabian scholar al Idrisi as early as 1150. From 1317 it was the capital of a separate duchy, which in 1456 was purchased by the Polish king Casimir Jagiellon and later (1564) incorporated into the Cracow voivodship. In the times of the Reformation, the town was the scene of violent religious struggles. After the first partition (1772) it was incorporated into Austria. A small industrial and trading town before the Second World War it is an important industrial and communication centre today.

The name Oświęcim (German name Auschwitz) is linked above all with the huge concentration camp set up there in 1940 during the Nazi occupation. Konzentrationslager Auschwitz-Birkenau was one of the most terrible death camps in which millions of people of 28 nationalities lost their lives, Poles and Jews constituting the great majority of prisoners. In memory of their martyrdom, the camp has been turned into a museum [64]. A monument has been built to commemorate those who died there. (I.J.K.)

64. Oświęcim (Auschwitz).
    Nazi concentration camp

Polish Uplands

The rich natural resources of the Silesian Upland led to the creation of the biggest mining and heavy industry district in Poland. The first written records of mining in Upper Silesia date back to the 12th century; it is known, however, that the mining and smelting of silver, lead and iron ores started much earlier. In the 18th century, zinc ores started being exploited, too. However, the development of mining and industry was connected with the main wealth of the Silesian Upland, namely hard coal. At the turn of the 18th and 19th century, two blast furnaces fired with coke, the first ones in Europe, were constructed here. Coal took on real importance in connection with the concentration of industry in the Coal Basin and the spontaneous development of towns. Villages grew into workers' settlements and new townships arose. Industrial agglomerations developed as these newer and older settlements merged with each other. Gradually, the area of the central coal basin became an urban-industrial conurbation known as the Upper Silesian Industrial District (Górnośląski Okręg Przemysłowy - GOP). Coal mining remains the main activity.

The main centre of this industrial-urban agglomeration is located in Katowice, the voivodship capital, an important railway junction and an economic and cultural centre of Upper Silesia. Katowice developed above all as a coal mining center, one of the oldest mines being "Kleofas", in operation since 1822 [67]. Katowice was granted municipal status in 1865. Poor workers' districts [68] grew up in the vicinity of the mines and factories to be partially replaced by postwar housing estates. The city centre is still undergoing redevelopment.

The heavy concentration of industry in the Upper Silesian Coal Basin has resulted in deleterious changes to the natural environment and living conditions of the inhabitants. No other part of Poland has become so severely polluted. Intensive mining, heavy industry and urban development have transformed the natural habitat, especially hydrographic conditions, soil and vegetation. The landscape is dominated by smoking chimneys, blast furnaces, mine shafts, coal tips and hollows created by mining. Coal dust and other pollutants from the factories reduce sunlight destroying natural vegetation and causing serious human ailments. The densely populated region suffers from chronic shortages of water, which is contaminated anyway. Countermeasures have been introduced in the form of replantation projects, new parks in the towns, recultivated coal tips and depresions, artificial reservoirs, etc. A protective forest belt has been planted around the conurbation. New housing estates have been raised beyond the coal basin. Industrial enterprises not directly connected with coal-mining, have been reduced within the

◁ 65. Landscape in the Kielce region

66. Upper Silesia. „Rydłutowy I" coal mine

conurbation itself and even located outside the coal basin. The power station in Łaziska Górne as well as Poland's most modern and largest steelworks, "Katowice", opened in 1978 [71], are two such cases. Following its modernization, "Katowice" is intended to take over the production of pig iron and steel from the old Upper Silesian steelworks which will be refurbished as manufacturing or processing plants with the aim of reducing pollution in the industrial area's heart. Little in this area has been achieved until now.

A number of older settlements has become part of the Upper Silesian conurbation, including Będzin which developed in the late Middle Ages on a trade route connecting Cracow and Wrocław. Będzin boasts a 13th century castle with a tower raised at the turn of the 13th century [75]. The castle was reconstructed after the Second World War to accommodate a regional museum.

The town of Pszczyna [69] lies beyond the Upper Silesian industrial area. A former ducal seat, Pszczyna has expanded to become an industry and service centre. A settlement was probably established here in the 10th century. The town's numerous owners included the Racibórz princes, Jagiellon kings, Cieszyn Piasts and the German Hochbergs von Pless. It was returned to Poland in 1921, and the Pszczyna princes, owners of vast tracts of rural land, coal mines and factories, were known to be among the richest families in Europe. The originally Gothic castle, erected on the site of an old Slavic fort, was completely rebuilt between 1743 and 1767, and again in 1870–1874. A museum of period interiors, exhibiting various examples of 19th century salons in accordance with changing tastes and the spirit of the times, was opened in 1945. The castle also possesses the loveliest park in all Silesia; on account of its ancient trees and rare flora, it has become a natural reserve. Aurochs were reintroduced to the Pszczyna woods in 1865. (I.J.K.)

Częstochowa is situated in the northern part of the Silesian Upland. It was created in 1826 of the unification of two previously separate towns, Stara Częstochowa on the River Warta and Częstochówka lying at the foot of Jasna Góra hill. A foundation charter was granted to Stara Częstochowa in 1356, although there are older references to both settlements dating to 1220. Prince Władysław Opolczyk, when granting his brothers, Jaśko and Niczko a foundry built in 1377 to exploit the rich iron ore deposits, referred to Stara Częstochowa as a town. Five years later he invited the Pauline brethren from Hungary,

67. Upper Silesia. „Kleofas" coal mine ▷

68. Katowice. City centre ▷

69. Pszczyna. Market place ▷

70. Silesian folk costumes ▷

providing them with monastery buildings raised next to a church on the Jasna Góra hill. A Byzantine portrait of the Madonna [73], which was to become a cult object drawing annually large numbers of pilgrims, was placed in the monastery church at that time. The monastery was successively rebuilt, and in 1620 it was strongly fortified according to new designs introduced from Italy [72]. The most famous defence occured during the Swedish invasion of 1655 when a small group of defenders succeeded in repulsing the attacks of the vastly superior invading forces. Annual pilgrimages greatly influenced the development of the crafts; Częstochówka developed largely as a settlement serving pilgrims' needs. It achieved municipal status in 1717 when it began to be known as Nowa Częstochowa. Industry evolved in Częstochowa after unification, and was particularly expanded following the Second World War, since when it has become one of the most important industrial cities in Poland. Textile manufacturing and metallurgy lead the field, continuing the 14th century foundry traditions, although there are numerous plants specialising in other branches.

The city continues to grow, new housing estates have appeared, together with two higher education institutes. Since 1975 Częstochowa has been a voivodship seat. Tourism inevitably focuses on the Jasna Góra monastery, a major monument of national culture and the largest religious and devotional centre in Poland. The monastery, having undergone a number of additions and conversions, is predominantly Baroque, including the richly decorated interiors. Among the many valuable religious relics housed there, special mention is due to fine objects of goldsmithery in the monastery treasury, book collections, the archives and a printing house operating since the 18th century. (I.J.K.)

During the reign of Casimir the Great many watchtowers and castles were constructed on the limestone hills of the Cracow-Częstochowa Uplands to guard the border with Silesia which had been lost to Bohemia. Today, an attractive tourist route known as the Eagle Nest Trail winds through the hills for about 160 km. Apart from the picturesque limestone residual rocks, the route offers historic monuments and natural wonders. Most of the castles are in ruins, the majority having been destroyed during the Swedish wars. The highest elevation in the Uplands (504 m) is crowned by the magnificent Gothic and Renaissance ruins of Ogrodzieniec Castle [76] raised in the years 1530–1545 for Seweryn Boner, treasurer to King Sigismund the Old. The castle, superbly designed and located on an escarpment, was torched by the Swedes and subsequently rebuilt in part. It was preserved in a relatively good state until the 19th century when it fell into ruin; the last war brought

71. „Katowice" steelworks

72. Częstochowa. Jasna Góra monastery

73. Częstochowa. Jasna Góra
monastery. Chapel with the
miraculous Holy Mother from
Częstochowa icon

74. Pszczyna. Palace interiors

76. Ogrodzieniec. Castle ruins

77. Tenczyn. Castle ruins

75. Będzin. Castle

about its total devastation. Efforts are being made by its present owner, the state, to reconstruct it to serve tourist purposes.

Ojców and its environs, now a national park, is considered to be the most beautiful part of the Cracow-Częstochowa Uplands. In the upper part of the deep River Prądnik valley stands Pieskowa Skała (Dog's Rock) Castle, built by Casimir the Great on a rocky promontory of that name. Originally a Gothic structure, it was reconstructed in the 16th century as a Renaissance residence [78] for the Szafraniec family. Following the ravages caused by the Swedish wars, the castle was rebuilt by the Zebrzydowski family. Towards the close of the 19th century, Pieskowa Skała, said to have been lost in a card game, was purchased with public donations and adapted for use as a holiday hotel. Valuable collections of Renaissance art are housed in the castle which was restored in the 1960s. The building consists of several sections and the original Gothic walls have survived in part, although the arcaded courtyard is the single most impressive feature [79]. Below the castle rises the Club of Hercules, a free-standing limestone rock created by weathering [78].

At Tenczyn, at the southern end of the Cracow-Częstochowa Uplands, imposing ruins of a 14th century castle once belonging to the Tenczyński, a powerful Małopolska family, rise from rocks created by prehistoric volcanic activity [77]. Originally Gothic, the castle was rebuilt in 1570 as a magnificent Renaissance residence. It fell into decay during the 18th century. (I.J.K.)

In a narrow gorge known as the Cracow Gate, separating the Cracow- Częstochowa Uplands and the Subcarpathians, Tyniec Abbey, a resplendent Bendictine complex, rises above the Vistula on limestone rocks [80]. According to the chronicles of Jan Długosz, the abbey was founded by Casimir the Restorer in 1044. The abbot of Tyniec was the superior of all Benedictine monasteries in Poland, Silesia and later Lithuania. The 11th century Romanesque basilica destroyed in 1241 by the Tartars was replaced in the 15th century by a Gothic church. The Gothic walls have remained in spite of extensive rebuilding in the Baroque style (1618–1622). Following the Benedictine Order's dissolution in 1817, the abbey passed to the Jesuits, although the Benedictines returned there shortly before the Second World War.

East of Tyniec, a 17th century Cameldolite church and monastery complex is surrounded by woodlands on the Srebrna skała of Bielany, today an outer suburb of Cracow [81].

78. Pieskowa Skała. Castle and Club of Hercules

79. Pieskowa Skała. Castle courtyard

80. Tyniec. Benedictine abbey

81. Cracow. Cameldolite monastery complex in Bielany

Cracow, Poland's former capital city, is a monument to the past, but at the same time it has become a large, modern city. It was most probably a centre for the Wiślanie tribes. Its name is assumed to derive from the legendary Prince Krak, who supposedly founded the town after slaying a dragon which had been living in the Wawel Cave. The legend goes on to tell of Krak's daughter, Wanda, who preferred to drown in the Vistula rather than marry a German prince and surrender her lands to him. Long before the foundation of the Polish state, there existed a stronghold on Wawel Hill. During the times of the first Piasts rulers, Wawel was a princely seat; then, during the breakdown into duchies, it became the seat of the Prince-senior. Following the reunification of the Polish lands, Wawel became the seat of Poland's monarchs until the late 16th century, continuing to serve as a royal residence until the Partitions [82, 83]. As early as the 10th century, Cracow had become a populous settlement situated on a major trade route between Prague and Kievan Ruthenia. Following its destruction by the Tartars in 1241, the town was completely rebuilt and organised anew according to a foundation charter from 1257. It was at this time that the regular street network of the Old Town was established, including the extensive Market Place, covering 4 hectares at the very centre. The Market Place was occupied by stalls, later replaced by the Cloth Hall. Burned down in the mid-16th century, the originally 14th century structure was rebuilt wih a fine Renaissance attic [91]. Only the lofty tower has remained of the 14th century town hall; the tower was given a Baroque crown in the 18th century [92]. In a corner of the Market Place stands the magnificent Gothic Church of St.Mary. Two small churches are also situated in the Market Place, the square itself being surrounded by old burghers' houses. (I.J.K.)

Late-medieval Cracow flourished to reach its zenith in the later half of the 15th and 16th century as a royal capital to the Jagiellon monarchy, a rapidly expanding power competing with the Habsburgs for a dominant position in Eastern Europe. When the capital was moved to Warsaw in 1596, as well as under the impact of political and economic crises from the mid-17th century on, Cracow's former spledour faded and disappeared. Following the Third Partition of Poland in 1795, it came under Austrian rule. The Congress of Vienna granted it free city status, but it was again incorporated into the Austrian Empire barely thirty years later in 1846. As a provincial town of the monarchy, it grew economically at a snail's pace, but always remained a key centre of Polish national and political life, especially the arts and sciences. In the Jagiellonian University, the oldest in Poland and one of Europe's oldest, founded in 1364 by Casimir the Great, Poles from all three partitions were able to study. Cracow was

82. Cracow. Wawel Castle

the birthplace of new schools of scientific thought, new literary trends and new styles in art. At the beginning of the 20th century, Cracow café "Jama Michalikowa" was the meeting place of artists and writers from all over Poland, while the renowned Słowacki Theatre, played a leading role in the country's theatrical life [99].

The quickened pace of urban growth was halted by the Second World War. Under German occupation, Cracow became the administrative capital of the so-called General Governorate. The city was looted and many of its treasures were shipped away. Nazi plans to blow up Wawel and other historical buildings before retreating were blocked by the brilliant Soviet army manoeuvre to take the city. Cracow was one of the few larger Polish cities to be spared serious damages to its architecture during the last war. Historical buildings are so great in number, it is impossible to enumerate even those of highest value.

Cracow has retained its importance as an educational and cultural centre. It has extended its tourist facilities while becoming extensively industrialized. (I.J.K.)

The most ancient vestiges of pre-Romanesque architecture to be discovered on Wawel Hill are most likely from the times of King Bolesław the Brave (i.e., the turn of the 10th century). The rotunda of St. Felix and St. Adault is well-preserved. The first Wawel cathedral was built a century later, already in a fully evolved Romanesque style. St. Leonard's crypt [87] as well as parts of the tower have survived of this structure. The Wawel complex which has come down to our times has retained its originally Gothic plan. The groundfloor castle chambers, defense walls and three-aisled main body of the cathedral are 14th and 15th century in date. The Renaissance style prevails, however, in Wawel's reconstruction dated to 1502–1536 following a disastrous fire during the reign of Sigismund the Old. Francesco of Florence, brought from Hungary for the project, concentrated on a three-storey arcaded courtyard featuring columned galleries [85]; it was completed under the guidance of Bartolomeo Berrecci. The royal castle interiors are richly decorated with painted frescoes, mosaic floors, coffered ceilings, decorative tiles, ornate furniture, valuable paintings [85], culminating in the famous tapestries made in Brussels on special commission from Sigismund Augustus (1550–1565). Berrecci also designed the Jagiellon Kings' mausoleum known as the Sigismund Chapel in 1517–1566 [86], one of the most sublime examples of mature Renaissance architecture to be found beyond the Italian peninsula. As a mausoleum, it became the model for countless burial chapels of magnates and the gentry constructed throughout the Polish and Lithuanian territories in the 16th and early 17th centuries. An impressive marble cupola on an elevated drum pierced by round windows [89] crowns it. Relief mythological scenes adorning the interior walls symbolise the soul's way to salvation, in accordance with Renaissance ideals. The

85. Cracow. Senators Chamber

86. Cracow.
Wawel cathedral

83. Cracow. Wawel hill. Northeastern
view

84. Cracow. Arcaded galleries in the
courtyard of Wawel Castle

87. Cracow. St. Leonard's crypt in Wawel cathedral

88. Cracow. St. Stanislas reliquary
in Wawel cathedral

coffers of the dome contain rosettes of varying designs.

Gothic royal tombs are placed in the cathedral aisles and chapels. The Wawel cathedral was the coronation church of the monarchs of Poland. The tomb of Władysław Jagiełło [90], presumably designed around 1430 when the king was still alive, received a Renaissance canopy designed in 1519–1524 by the Italians Giovanni Cini and Berrecci, founded by the king's grandson, Sigismund the Old.

A sculptural masterpiece from the end of the Middle Ages, the tomb of Casimir Jagiellon, carved in marble by Veit Stoss around 1492, was placed in the Holy Cross chapel. This chapel, richly ornamented with an Old Ruthenian-Byzantine polychromy from the 15th century, is a rare phenomenon outside the Orthodox world. The Baroque sarcophagus of St.Stanislas dating from 1669–1671 [88] stands in the main aisle. A silver coffin, supported by angels and displaying scenes from the bishop's life, is the work of a Gdańsk artist of Flemish background, Peter van der Rennen. The coffin is placed under a canopy with a cupola conceived somewhat earlier by the royal architect, Giovanni Batista Travano, a leading artist working in Poland during the earlier half of the 17th century.

Cracow's medieval town walls were largely demolished in the early 19th century. Three bastions, the Florian Gate and a barbican [114] raised in the late 15th century as an additional defence and a precaution against Turkish-Ottoman invasion, have been preserved. Cracow's Barbican is a rare survivor of this type of late-medieval architecture; two parallel defensive walls originally connected it with the Florian Gate. (P.T.)

The St.Mary church [92] popularly known as "Mariacki church", was the Cracow burghers' church and was raised in the 13th century on the Main Market Place. The present building, dating from 1355–1365, is a three-aisled Gothic basilica with a twin tower façade. The loftier tower, from which the medieval "hejnał" (bugle call) is still sounded daily, possesses a highly original Late-Gothic crown of 1478; that of the lower tower was completed in 1592. The richly embellished interiors received a new polychromy whose author was Jan Matejko in 1889–1891. Placed against Gothic stained glass windows and occupying the entire presbytery, the late Gothic altarpiece [93] is a triptych which was carved in wood by the great Nuremberg artist Veit Stoss between 1477 and 1489. The open altar is dominated by a scene representing the laying to rest of the Virgin Mary, above which the artist conceived interpretations of the *Assumption* and *Coronation*, surmounted by a delicate canopy. The altar rests on a predella portraying the Madonna's genealogical tree. Bas-

89. Cracow. Sigismund Chapel in the cathedral

90. Cracow. King Władysław Jagiełło's tomb in Wawel cathedral

91. Cracow. Market Square

92. Cracow. Market Square, Cloth Hall and Church of St. Mary

93. Cracow. Altar in the Church of St. Mary

reliefs in the side wings present scenes from the *Annunciation* to the *Pentecost*. The closed triptych reveals twelve scenes from the lives of Christ and the Virgin Mary. During the last war, the Nazis removed the altar to Nuremberg, but it was returned in 1946. A stone crucifix also by Veit Stoss is a work of outstanding and harmonious beauty. (P.T.)

In 1364, Casimir the Great founded the Cracow University, greatly enhancing the city's status as a centre of learning. The oldest university building, the Collegium Maius, was constructed in the 15th century by combining a number of older houses. The 15th century proved to be a golden era for the university; the intellectual ferment arose in part from the Renaissance, while academic advances were accelerated from the 1470s by breakthroughs in printing techniques. Cracow's reputation for its achievements in astronomy, law, theology and aesthetics attracted people from all parts of Central and Eastern Europe. The courtyard [95] from the turn of the 15th and 16th centuries with its characteristic stellar vaulting and galleries, is embellished with sculptures belonging to the original university buildings. A series of reading rooms decorated with paintings is located on the first floor. According to tradition, Dr. Faust from Goethe's drama was supposed to have studied here. Nicholas Copernicus, John of Glogau, Marcin Bylica and other great scholars studied here for certain. Priceless collections belonging to the University Museum were amassed over the centuries, starting with Marcin Bylica's astronomical instruments donated to the university in 1491. (P.T.)

Palatine Sieciech, an active and influential figure in the Duchy of Władysław Herman, was responsible for founding the church of St. Andrew near his residential seat in the settlement of Okół lying below Wawel Hill [96]. A unique example of Polish Romanesque art, representing all the main elements of a monumental basilica in smaller scale, the church has three aisles and a transept, but only a single bay. Two high towers with windows dominate the western facade. The overall effect of this medieval stone edifice is one of refined lightness.
In the 14th century Casimir the Great founded an autonomous town which took his name: Kazimierz. Located outside the town, it numbered in those times about 3000 inhabitants, the vast majority of whom were Jewish. At the end of the 15th century, King Jan Olbracht had all of Cracow's Jewish community settled here.

94. Cracow. Barbican and Florian Gate

95. Cracow. Courtyard of Collegium Maius

96. Cracow. Church
of St. Andrew

97. Cracow. Church of St. Ann

98. Cracow. Synagogue interior

Kazimierz was incorporated into the main city in 1791. In spite of the destruction caused during the last war, and the murder of most of its inhabitants, Kazimierz has preserved many relics of Poland's Jewish heritage, including the Remuh cemetery and a number of synagogues, of which the oldest [98] comes from the late 14th century and was rebuilt by Santi Gucci at the end of the 16th century. The Museum of Jewish History, Culture and Martyrdom is housed in the so-called Old Synagogue.

The interiors of St.Anne's church [97] constitute one of the most valuable examples of Baroque art in Poland.The building was erected in 1689–1704 by the Dutch artist Tylman from Utrecht. Ennobled in Poland, he was its most accomplished architect in the second half of the 17th century. The façade relates to picturesque, chiaroscuro forms of the Roman Baroque. The architect took full account of the street's narrowness and compensated for it. A number of gifted artists designed the interiors: the Italian Baltasare Fontana executed the superb stuccos, while the frescoes are by Karl and Innocenti Monti and Karol Dankwart, with two Polish designers, Jerzy Siemiginowski and Szymon Czechowicz, being responsible for the altar paintings. These exceptionally uniform interiors present an attempt through Italian Baroque forms and stunning richness to achieve a synthesis of all the fine arts. (P.T.)

Cracow possesses more than a score of museums preserving documents from 1000 years of Polish history. Six branches of the National Museum display what is perhaps the richest collection of Polish art from the Middle Ages to modern times, works of the European masters, including Leonardo da Vinci and Rembrandt, valuable arms and a collection of Japanese art. (P.T)

The chapel-mausoleum of the Firlejs in Bejsce [100] offers a good example of how artistic patronage operated in Renaissance Poland. The mausoleum's exuberant decor is deprived of harmony and moderation, and intensified by a variety of forms; it is an expression of *horror vacui* associated with mannerist art. The photograph fails to give a full impression of the decoration's dynamic qualities, breaking down this small building's architectural structure, reflecting the mannerist love of the fantastic and its refusal to be limited. The artist responsible for the chapel (1593–1601) belonged to the circle of Santi Gucci. The founder, Mikołaj Firlej, voivode of Cracow, looked to the Sigismund Chapel on Wawel for his model. Firlej, brought up as a Calvinist, became a fervent Catholic after his travels to Italy in 1569. His tomb

99. Cracow. Słowacki theatre and St. Cross church

100. Bejce. Firlej chapel interior, fragment of a tomb ▷

101. Wiślica. Collegiate church interior ▷

presents him kneeling, in accordance with the post-Tridentine spirit of devotion, before the crucifix. He was a prominent statesman of the post-Jagiellon period, well-educated and possibly the first true archeologist in Poland to carry out excavations.

Casimir the Great is commonly known to have "inherited a wooden Poland and left it built in stone". Indeed, he erected many castles and churches, including the collegiate church in Wiślica [101]. A Gothic temple of delicate proportions, it was raised in the late 14th century and consists of a two-aisled hall, elongated presbytery and exquisitely traced tripartite ribbed vaulting. The Old Ruthenian-Byzantine polychromy reflects the tastes of the later patron, king Władysław Jagiełło.

Investigations under the church floor uncovered the crypt of a Romanesque temple. On the earlier beautifully-patterned floor symbolic creatures are presented, together with a tree of life, protected by lions and other figures referring to the ruler of these lands in the early 12th century, prince Henryk of Sandomierz and his family. The Latin script expresses humility and hope for eternal salvation. It is one of the most interesting examples of Romanesque art in Europe. (P.T.)

To the northeast of Cracow, as far as the Nida Basin, there stretch the fertile and picturesque Miechów Uplands, which are considered to have been one of the earliest areas of settlement in Poland.

The site of marble quarries and a food processing centre, Pińczów on the River Nida [102], has become a popular tourist attraction (an artificial lake, interesting surroundings, tourist and hiking trails). In the 11th and 12th centuries, vineyards grew in the vicinity of the township. In 1429, the town received municipal status from bishop Zbigniew Oleśnicki, who built a castle, collegiate church and Pauline monastery. In the 16th century, Pińczów became a leading centre of the Polish Reformation movement as the main base of the Polish Brethren, also known as the Arian Brothers. An important cultural and intellectual centre, it came to be known as the "Sarmatian Athens". When the Polish Brethren were forced into exile, the town declined. It was almost completely destroyed in September 1939, although its historic urban layout was retained in the post-war reconstruction. (I.J.K.)

102. Pińczów

103. Chęciny. Castle ruins

104. Świętokrzyskie Mountains. „Raj" cave

105. Kielce. Bishop's palace

The Chęciny Chain, forming the southern fringe of the Świętokrzyskie Mountains, is marked from a distance by the ruins of Chęciny Castle [103], built in the years 1296–1306. It was one of the most important defensive strongholds in late-medieval Poland, and also a place where the nobility would hold its assemblies. Badly damaged during the Swedish wars, it fell into ruin. At the foot of the castle there is the historic small town of Chęciny which used to be an important lead and copper mining as well as stone-quarrying settlement in the 15th–18th centuries. A small but very attractive grotto known as "Raj" (Paradise) [104] was discovered in the vicinity. (I.J.K.)

The chief town of the Świętokrzyskie Mountain region is Kielce, pleasantly located in a dale. The town developed from a trading and market centre, already mentioned in 11th century chronicles. It became the property of the bishops of Cracow at the end of that century, and operated for a long time as a centre for the church estates. In 1364, it was granted municipal rights on the basis of the Magdeburg Law. In the 15th to 17th centuries, it experienced dynamic growth due to the development of mining and the processing of lead, copper and iron ores in the surrounding area. It was at this time that the beautiful, early-Baroque Episcopal Palace [105] was built (1637–1641) by Bishop Jakub Zadzik. The interior polychromy has been preserved together with ornate ceilings, paintings, portals and fireplaces. The neighbouring cathedral, following extensive rebuilding in 1632–1635, took on the character of an early-Baroque basilica. Kielce became Crown property in 1789. From 1816 it was a voivodship capital, later the seat of a Russian governorate. In 1816 Stanisław Staszic opened the Mining Academy here while expanding the existing Mining Board in connection with the region's growing coal and iron-smelting industries. The decline of the industrial area in the mid-19th century, as well as the transferring of the administration to Radom, seriously undermined the town's urban development. Renewed activity came with the railway line opened at the end of the 19th century, connecting Kielce with Dąbrowa Górnicza, Częstochowa and Warsaw. Voivodship town status was returned after 1918. The industry was greatly expanded in concordance with postwar policies. Kielce still remains an attractive city for its location in the heart of the Świętokrzyskie Mountains. Tourists are attracted by folk dresses put on during holidays and important family occassions. The dresses were usually quite expensive and were passed on from generation to generation. Having such a dress was not as important as knowing how to wear it. [111].

106. Świętokrzyskie Mountains

The Świętokrzyskie Mountains [106]
rise above the characteristically flat
Małopolska Uplands. The mountains
consist of abrupt slopes and post-
-glacial boulderfields known as *gołobo-
rze*, as well as inselbergs and deeply
incised valleys. After the Sudetens,
these are the oldest mountains in Poland, characterized by a well-preserved
fold structure. The central mountain
chain gives way to more than a dozen
subsidiary chains of similar altitude.
This core is composed of the Łysogóra
and Dymińskie chains. The Świętokrzyskie range, and particularly the
Łysogóra chain, is characterised by its
own microclimate reflected in lower
average temperatures, more abundant
rainfalls and a shorter growing season.
The mountain chains are covered with
thick fir, larch and beech forests. Ancient vegetation has survived in the
peatbogs from the Ice Age, while pine
woods grow on the lower mountain
levels becoming mixed with other species higher up. The most valued parts of
the Łysogóra chain have been turned
into a national park. Loess uplands lie
along the foothills and stretch to the
east. The highest peaks belong to the
Łysogóra chain: Łysica (612 m) [107],
also known as St.Katarzyna, composed
of twin peaks and a large boulderfield,
and Łysa Góra (595 m), also known as
the Holy Cross (Święty Krzyż) or Ła-
siec, with the largest single quartz ridge
[108]. Łysa Góra was a major meeting
place for pagan tribes who held their
religious ceremonies there; a sanctuary
wall (1.2 km) encircling the peak has
survived, while legends abound about
witches sabbats taking place there.
A Benedictine abbey was built here in
1103 and remained open until 1818.
The abbey complex [109] consists of
buildings arranged around a central
square court: arcaded Gothic cloisters
(14th–15th centuries), an early-Baroque chapel (17th century) and a Baro-
que-cum-Neo-Classical church (18th
century). The monastery is surrounded
by dark fir forests. [110] (I.J.K.).

The Świętokrzyskie Mountains and
their surroundings were the cradle of
mining and metallurgical activities
reaching back to ancient times. Copper,
iron and lead ores were mined here two
thousand years ago. In Roman times
(2nd and 3rd centuries AD) one of the
largest iron foundries in Europe operated here, producing tools, weapons and
nails. Furnaces for smelting iron were
developed in the 15th and 16th centuries. Water power from the rivers and
streams was used to move the forge
wheels and the furnaces were fired with
wood. In 1598 the first smelting furnace
fired with charcoal was put into operation at Samsonów and proved with time
to be considerably more productive
than the original ones. Blast furnaces
were developed in the 18th century.

107. Świętokrzyskie Mountains.
Łysica peak

108. Świętokrzyskie Mountains.
Łysica peak

109. Świętokrzyskie Mountains.
Monastery on Mt. Holy Cross

110. Świętokrzyskie Mountains. Fir Wood

111. Świętokrzyskie Mountains. Folk costumes

112. Świętokrzyskie Mountains. Ruins of the great furnace in Samsonów

113. Świętokrzyskie Mountains. Water dam in Nietulisko

115. Szydłowiec. Town hall

116. Szydłowiec. Jewish monastery

114. Świętokrzyskie Mountains. Ancient oak tree „Bartek”

Blacksmiths forges, tinsmith workshops and workshops making axes and pipes grew up around the furnaces. The Staropolskie Industrial District experienced its greatest growth during the 1820s and 1830s when planned industrialisation was undertaken by the autonomous authorities of the Polish Congress Kingdom. Much capital was put into the iron industry's expansion on the banks of the Kamienna, Bobrza and Czarna rivers. Iron works established upstream supplied those operating further down the rivers with raw materials. Following the November Uprising the industry continued to be financially supported by the Polish Bank (until 1845). Many examples of old industrial buildings have remained from this period. The ruins of a smelting furnace still exist in Samsonów [112], while in Nietulisko there are ruins of a dam [113], as well as a rolling mill, industrial works, administrative buildings and a workers' housing estate in Sielpia Wielka. Most of the early-19th century industrial buildings in this region ceased operation in the later part of the 1800s when charcoal-burning foundries became obsolete, owing to the introducion of a new fuel, coal. Ostrowiec and Starachowice, connected by railway to the Dąbrowa Górnicza coal basin, were the only two centres able to continue operating.

The Staropolskie Industrial District has become an additional tourist attraction in the Świętokrzyskie Mountains. The area can also boast some natural wonders; among others the ancient oak tree Bartek [114] near Samsonów which is one of the oldest trees in Poland, estimated to be more than 1000 years old. The circumference of its trunk is 13.4 m.

Szydłowiec lies on the northeastern edge of the Świętokrzyskie Mountains; from the Middle Ages it has served as a center of sandstone quarrying. The surviving historic monuments include the castle of the Szydłowiecki family (16th century, rebuilt in the following century by the Radziwiłłs), a parish dating from the turn of the 14th century, and a late-Renaissance town hall [115] constructed in 1602–26. A rare vestige of the past is a Jewish cemetery with tombstones dating from the 18th and 19th centuries. (I.J.K.)

In the years 1627–1644, near the present day village of Ujazd, the Italian architect Lorenzo Senes built a castle called Krzyżtopór for Krzysztof Ossoliński [119]. With its exceptional artistic program and immense scale it is surely one of the most individualistic architectural monuments on the European subcontinent. Plundered and burned by the Swedes in 1655, it functioned for barely 11 years, a proud and symbolic manifestation of the Sarmatian pride and love of opulence. With its regular pentagonal bastions surrounded by a moat, it was intended to re-

present the Ossoliński family's continuity, possessing as many towers as seasons, chambers as months, rooms as weeks and windows as days in the year. The castle's façade received a colourful sgrafitto, including zodiac signs and a genealogical tree reaching back, in accordance with Sarmatian ideology, to ancient Rome. The palace complex was traversed by a small road leading to a four-storeyed and arcaded eliptical courtyard. The arcaded courtyard passageways led into sumptuous chambers reaching 10 m in height with windows about 7 m high. The largest bastion accommodated a hall with the most unexpected surprise: an elevated aquarium with tropical fish in the place of a ceiling. The castle, which took its name from the great coat–of–arms above the entrance gate – a cross ("krzyż") and axe ("topór"), represents a superb combination of western mannerism and the ideals of Polish Sarmatism.

In the years 1643–1650 the same architect designed a second unusual building for Jerzy Ossoliński: the collegiate church in Klimontów [118]. The elliptical nave is surrounded on the inside by two-storeyed vaulted galleries with breaks in the walls to permit the church to be viewed on each level. As in Krzyżtopór, the architect revealed his skill in creating a beautiful piece of architecture for art's sake, typical of mannerism in its lack of functional justification.

The town walls [120], castle and church at Szydłów date back to the days of Casimir the Great, constituting a well-preserved complex of Gothic architecture and town planning from the mid-14th century. (P.T.)

Sandomierz [121, 122], the capital of the Sandomierz Uplands with the deep wooded ravines, is picturesquely situated on the Vistula. It is one of the most beautiful towns in Poland with origins going back to the 8th–9th century. In the times of Bolesław the Brave, an important stronghold existed here, which following the country's feudal division became a ducal capital and then, when the country was reunited, the seat of a voivodship. Situated at the crossroads of routes from Hungary and Ruthenia, the town was frequently raided by the Ruthenians, Lithuanians and Tartars. Prince Leszek the White built a castle in 1200–1207 and municipal status was granted in 1286 by Leszek the Black, together with a number of trading privileges. Casimir the Great enclosed the town with a defence wall and rebuilt the castle as well as the small town hall. Church and public buildings were erected. Like most of Poland's historic towns, Sandomierz enjoyed its

117. Wąchock. Chapterhouse of the Cistercian abbey

118. Klimontów. Collegiate church

greatest prosperity in the 15th, 16th and early 17th centuries. It took advantage of the Vistula trade route opened in the 15th century; numerous grain warehouses were constructed along the waterfront. The town declined after Poland's partition. Its economic position did not improve until the 1930s when it became part of the Central Industrial Region created by the Polish government. Fortunately spared destruction in the last war, Sandomierz has become an important tourist centre.

The oldest building in Sandomierz is the brick church of St.James, originating from 1226 and forming part of the Dominican monastery. The present cathedral was founded as a collegiate church in 1360; it contains well-preserved Old Ruthenian-Byzantine frescoes from the 15th century. The 15th century house of Jan Długosz, the famous Polish chronicler, is located near the cathedral. Only the west wing with two Gothic towers has remained of the old castle. In the large Market Place, surrounded by old town houses [123], there is a very fine town hall, built in the mid-14th century, later remodelled in the Renaissance style. On the high bank of the Vistula there is the only surviving wing of the Renaissance Jesuit College, the so-called Gostomianum, founded in 1605–1615, in which the oldest grammar school for nobles was set up in Poland. The entire Old Town quarter surrounded by the partly preserved 14th century ramparts with the Opatów Gate constitutes a valuable complex of Romanesque, Gothic and Renaissance architecture and town-planning.

Loess ravines abound in the local countryside, among others the Queen Jadwiga Ravine [124], about 400m long, cutting deeply into the undersoil. (I.J.K.)

The Cistercian monks played an important part in the evolution of architecture in the Polish lands in the first half of the 13th century. Their stone monasteries and churches featured the earliest examples of cross-ribbed vaulting based on columns and pointed arches. All Cistercian complexes followed a similar plan and spatial design. The Kielce region monasteries of Wąchock [117], Koprzywnica and Sulejów repeat the model of the Fontenay Abbey in France, consisting of a three-aisled basilica with transepts and a towerless façade. The adjoining monastery complex to the south is centered around a square courtyard. The Cistercian abbey was a breakthrough in architectural design and building techniques of the Gothic style, occurring in Poland from the mid-13th century. (P.T.)

119. Ujazd. Ruins of the Krzyżtopór castle.

120. Szydłów. Cracow Gate

121. Vistula river near Sandomierz ▷

122. Sandomierz

123. Sandomierz. Town hall

124. Sandomierz Upland.
Jadwiga ravine

The Lublin Uplands is a gently rolling countryside with a network of river valleys, hills and shallow ravines. The fertile soils encouraged the development of agriculture. Industry is mainly connected with food processing and has been developed here only recently.

The historic town of Kazimierz Dolny, on the western border of the Lublin Uplands, in the Vistula Valley, is beautifully situated amid loess ravines [125]. It is one of the most charming spots in Poland, quite unique as regards its architecture and landscape, and an important leisure and tourist centre. The white buildings around the Market Place are concentrated at a point where the Vistula forms steeply sloping, green escarpments; they give way to houses lining streets which run up- and downhill, branching out in all directions over the width of the valley among orchards and stretching down to the water's edge. Above the houses nestling in the valley there rise the towers of old churches, above which there are the white ruins of a castle and watchtower perched on a hill. Kazimierz has been a favourite haunt of artists and writers since the 19th century.

The town's name is generally associated with Casimir the Great. An 11th century village belonging to the Norbertine nuns of Zwierzyniec near Cracow became a parish seat in 1315. The settlement at this time was called Kazimierz, suggesting it had already received its name during the reign of Prince Casimir the Just in the 12th century. The fact nevertheless remains that it was Casimir the Great who granted the town municipal status and built a fortified castle there.

The town's fortuitous position favoured its growth. A crossing point across the Vistula existed here on the trade route from Lvov to Silesia and Wielkopolska. This trade route became particularly important in the 16th century, while at this time a second route between Ruthenia and Prussia was opened. In addition, the Vistula grain trade began to flourish from the late Middle Ages and from the 16th century Kazimierz became an important loading port for the Lublin Uplands region. At this time the granaries were built [128]. The grain trade made merchant fortunes; richly ornamented merchants houses, that of the Przybyła family [126] and the house known as "Celejowska" [127] for example, survive to this day. The period of prosperity ended in the mid-17th century, when the country's political, social and economic situation took a decisive turn for the worse. A certain degree of activity returned in the late 19th century when the town began attracting artists and tourists. The beautiful scenery and remarkable architecture made Kazimierz a popular summer resort.

Ravaged in the Second World War, the town was painstakingly restored. New buildings were designed to harmonise

127. Kazimierz Dolny. „Celejowska" town house

128. Kazimierz Dolny. Granary

with the town's unique architecture. Holiday homes, pensions and hostels have been constructed to accommodate the increasing numbers of domestic and foreign visitors. (I.J.K.)

Lublin has been the main centre of the Lublin Uplands since the 12th century and is situated on the River Bystrzyca, a tributary of the Wieprz, amid gently rolling hills. The town grew from a stronghold on the Polish-Ruthenian border and was destroyed many times by Ruthenian and Lithuanian invaders. It was granted municipal status in 1317. Casimir the Great built a castle there, encircled the town with defence walls and granted numerous privileges. Trade with Lithuania and Ruthenia thrived. Polish-Lithuanian councils, meetings and Diet assemblies were held here, as well as the signing of the union between Poland and Lithuania in 1569. The Crown Tribunal was established there in 1578. The Cossack and Swedish wars, plagues and fires ushered in the town's decline. In the 19th century Lublin was a government seat, a fact which brought revival, intensified after 1877 by the railway line and accompanying industrialisation. The first Polish government after the period of partitions was set up here on 7th November 1918. New factories and cultural institutions were opened during the interwar years. Lublin suffered extensive damages and heavy loss of life during the Second World War. Following its liberation in July 1944 and until Warsaw was freed in January 1945, Lublin operated as the capital of Poland. The first higher school to be opened in postwar Poland was the Maria Skłodowska-Curie University of Lublin. At present, the city is the major economic, academic and cultural centre in southeastern Poland. It possesses many old buildings, restored after wartime damages, particularly the Old Town where most of these monuments are concentrated. Of greatest interest are the town hall, erected in the 13th century, repeatedly renovated and enlarged, the last time in 1781; Renaissance and Baroque town houses; parts of the old defence walls with three gates; and the Dominican church dating back to 1342, which having undergone many alterations now has a Renaissance character, with Baroque towers and some elements of the older Gothic building. The cathedral, a former Jesuit church built in 1586–1603, is a beautiful example of Renaissance architecture, with a Classicist portico designed by Antonio Corazzi in 1819. Several monastery complexes constructed in the 15th to 17th centuries are located outside the Old Town. The castle [130] rises on a hill above the Old Town. All that

125. Kazimierz Dolny

126. Kazimierz Dolny. Przybyła family townhouses

129. Lublin

130. Lublin. Castle

131. Lublin. Monument to Victims
of Nazism in Majdanek

remains of the original castle built by Casimir the Great are the tower and Gothic Holy Trinity Chapel from the second half of the 14th century. The castle was completely rebuilt during the 19th century in the Neo-Gothic style. At Majdanek, a suburb of Lublin, the Nazis set up an extermination camp in 1941. The gas chambers claimed the lives of at least 360,000 persons of 51 nationalities (mostly Jews and Poles). A Martyrological Museum was opened on the site of the camp [131]. (I.J.K.)

The Post-Piarist church interiors in Chełm [132] represent an example of late-Baroque design from the first half of the 18th century. By this time Rome and her architectural monuments had ceased to serve as a model. The architects of Austria, southern Germany and Bohemia proposed new, complicated spatial arrangements, combining axial with central plans. Paolo Fontana, an architect from northern Italy, designed a number of buildings in this spirit. The Chełm temple's nave is based on a plan close to an ellipse with vaulting concealed by an illusionistic polychromy from 1758. The interior decoration is overwhelmingly Rococo. In 1579, the Venetian, Bernardo Morando drew up plans of a new town for the Royal Chancellor Jan Zamoyski, a renowned Polish statesman educated at the universities of Paris, Rome and Padua, Zamość was conceived as a stronghold and landed estate. In 1595, Zamoyski founded the Zamość Academy, a branch of the Jagiellonian University in Cracow. The town plan, based on the regular new towns created in Italy, has largely survived. Zamość was encircled by the new Italian-type defence walls with bastions and a moat. The town hall from the years 1639–1651 [134] occupies a central position with façades broken up into delicate details dwarfed by an immense segmented tower. The resulting effect of contrast and incohesion is typical of Mannerism and is stamped also on the collegiate church dating from 1587–1600. The interior [133], unlike Renaissance temples, is based on the contrasts of a high main aisle and a low, elongated presbytery. The geometrically patterned stucco lintels decorating the vaulting are typical of early-17th century Polish Mannerism.
The architecture of Zamość, though modelled on Italian forms, no longer had much to do with early 17th century Italian Renaissance, just as Zamoyski, a propagator of the Counter Reformation, was no longer an exemplary Renaissance humanist. (P.T.)

132. Chełm. Post-Piarist church interior

134. Zamość. Town hall and houses

133. Zamość. Collegiate church interior

136. Karkonosze. Mt. Śnieżka

137. Karkonosze. ,,The Pilgrims''
rock group

◁ 135. Karkonosze

138. Karkonosze. Little Lake

139. Karkonosze. Karpacz, ▷
the Wang temple

The highest massif of the Sudeten Mountains is the Karkonosze [135], a mainly granite range. The Karkonosze ridge ranges from 1300 to 1400 m in altitude; very few peaks rise above this ridge. Śnieżka is the highest [136] at 1602 m. At the top there is a meteorological station and a tourist shelter. Excellent views of the Sudeten may be appreciated from this point; on a clear night the lights of Prague lying some 80 km to the southeast are visible. The climate is severe; snow on Śnieżka lies an average of 194 days annually. A specific feature of the Karkonosze Mountains are the numerous scattered groups of rocks, some of them taking on weird and fantastic shapes, including a group known as the Pilgrims [137]. Mountain lakes occupy the post-glacial dales, where some ancient plant species have survived. The Mały Staw lake is surrounded by steep mountain slopes rising up to 200 m [138].

Karpacz, located below Mt.Śnieżka, was founded in the 14th century as a settlement for speculators in gold and semi-precious stones. In the 17th century it became known as a place where herbs collected in the surrounding forests were made into medicines. Since the mid-19th century it has grown to become one of the largest health centres and leisure resorts in the Sudeten. Tourists also use its facilities as a base for excursions into the surrounding mountains. A special feature of Karpacz is the so-called Wang temple [139], a wooden church dating from the early 13th century with richly adorned interiors. It was shipped here in the 19th century from the small Norwegian town of Wang and reconstructed and enlarged on the spot. (I.J.K.)

The main urban centre in the extensive Jelenia Góra Basin is Jelenia Góra itself, originally a settlement attached to a fortified castle founded in the years 1108–1111 by king Bolesław Krzywousty and located on the River Kamienna's left bank. It received municipal status most probably in the 13th century, when it had already become a large trading town. In the 14th and 15th centuries mining and iron smelting were developed, together with glass production and weaving, the latter taking a leading position in the town's economic life from the 16th to the 18th century. The finest materials, such as batiste and voile, not produced anywhere else in Silesia, were made here, while the largest cotton fabric markets were held in Jelenia Góra attracting buyers from most of the important European markets. Polished crystal glassware evolved out of the late-medieval glass production. Following the town's incorporation into Prussia in 1740, its economic development was checked and the weaving trade rapidly declined in the 19th century. A new period of development associated with textile mills and the rise of the ceramics

140. Jelenia Góra. Part of the Market Square

141. Jelenia Góra. Evangelistic church interiors

and paper industries came in the later part of the 19th century. Its industries have been expanded since 1945, while the town itself has become an important administrative and educational centre. It is also a base for tourists visiting the Western Sudeten ranges. The spa of Cieplice Zdrój and the Old Town's historic character heighten Jelenia Góra's attraction as a tourist centre. Many historic monuments attest to the town's period of prosperity. The charming Market Square lies at the heart of the old medieval quarter and is surrounded by arcaded Baroque town houses from the 17th and 18th centuries. The centrally-placed town hall comes from the 16th century, although enlarged in the 17th, and is fronted by an ornamental fountain with a statue of Neptune [140]. Jelenia Góra was an important centre of the Reformation: a Protestant school was set up here at the time and was reputed for its high teaching standards; later, however, it was taken over by the Jesuits during the Habsburg-imposed Counter Reformation. The Evangelical church (1709–1718), containing galleries and loggias for the accommodation of 400 people with an organ mounted above the main altar, is testimony to the town's Protestant traditions [141]. The Austrian emperor agreed to the church's erection under pressure from the Swedish king. It was a Swedish architect, Frantz of Reval (Tallin) who designed the temple in Jelenia Góra, drawing inspiration for it from St. Catherine's church in Stockholm. The town's theatre is an important cultural institution responsible for the international performances regularly taking place in the streets of Jelenia Góra. (I.J.K.)

On the borderline between the Kaczawskie and Izerskie Foothills, on the River Bóbr, there is Lwówek Śląski, one of Silesia's oldest towns, initially developing thanks to local gold and silver deposits. Municipal status was granted in 1209 by Prince Henry the Bearded who for a brief period ruled much of the Polish lands. Situated on a trade route leading from Germany through Wrocław and Cracow to Ruthenia, Lwówek began to prosper, especially in the 16th and early 17th century in connection with handicrafts, particularly linen and woollen cloth manufacturing. This town, one of the most populous in Silesia, was almost completely destroyed during the Thirty Years War. In spite of a certain revival afterwards, the town never regained its former splendour. Heavily destroyed at the close of the last war, Lwówek lost many of its historic monuments, although the Gothic church with its beautiful portal, the Gothic-Renaissance town hall with vaulted entrance hall [143] as well as parts of the defence walls have remain-

142. Lwówek Śląski. Town houses

143. Lwówek Śląski. Town hall vestibule

144. Strzegom. St. Peter and Paul church

ed along with Renaissance and Baroque houses erected in the 16th and 18th centuries [142].

The highest peak in the Kaczawskie Foothills is Ostrzyca [145] (499 m), a basalt mountain representing the vestiges of an extinct volcano. The mountain slopes are covered with rich deciduous forests and in parts with rocky debris. This characteristic vegetation and rock forms are under protection in the Ostrzyca natural reserve.

To the east of the Kaczawskie Foothills, on the River Nysa Szalona, there is Bolków, a former trading settlement, today a small industrial town and tourist centre. The town nestles at the foot of green schists, on top of which there stands one of the most strongly fortified castles in Silesia [146], built at the end of the 13th century by Prince Bolko I. The town took its name from this prince, who acted as its benefactor. The castle is connected with the town's defence walls. In spite of a number of fires and the damage inflicted by the Hussites and the Thirty Years War, Bolków has retained it medieval layout and historical character. The northern side of the Market Place is fronted by 16th and 17th century town houses with arcades. The castle, enlarged in the 14th and 16th centuries, fell into ruin during the 19th century. A regional museum is located in the northern, better preserved part of the castle. The castle tower provides an excellent view over the town and surrounding countryside. Mt.Ślęża (718 m), known also as Sobótka, in the 8th to 11th centuries was the site of pagan ceremonies held by the Ślężanie tribe, from whom the name of Silesia is derived. The mountain top was surrounded by a stone wall, the remains of which can be seen today along with the stone sculptures of tribal cult. [147]. (I.J.K.)

In the 14th century Silesia, politically fragmented into small principalities, became a fief of Bohemia. Attempts by Casimir the Great to reunite the province with the Polish Kingdom came to nothing. Only the Duchy of Jawór-Świdnica retained its independence until the end of the century. This political re-orientation placed Silesia within the artistic orbit of Prague and Vienna, a fact clearly revealed in the Gothic SS. Peter and Paul church at Strzegom [144], originating from the late 14th century. The church was raised by the Order of St.John according to a virtually complete plan for one of the great cathedrals. Richly sculptured portals refer in style to the Prague workshop of the Parler family. An interpretation of the Last Judgement adorns

145. Kaczawskie Foothills. Mt. Ostrzyca

146. Bolków. Castle and part of the Market Square

147. Ślęża. Pagan cult sculpture

the canopy, while in the tympanum there are scenes depicting the life and conversion of St.Paul.

The parish church in Świdnica, a Gothic basilica rebuilt in the 16th century on a central plan, comes from the same period. The nave is closed by the original main altar [148]. The circular construction surmounted on seven columns with a rich coping, designed by Johann Riedel in 1690–1694, is intended to symbolise the Old Testament House of Wisdom or Throne of Solomon. Most of the interior design comes from the 18th century when the local sculptor Georg Leonard Weber introduced holy figures on the church piers and designed the Heavenly Orchestra decorating the organ.

Following the Treaty of Westphalia, the Catholic authorities consented to the Silesian Protestants erecting three churches, on the conditions that they were built outside the towns. One such temple was built outside the Old Town of Świdnica in 1656 [149]; its vast interior can accommodate up to 3500 seated devotees thanks to a brilliantly executed plan. The interior ornamentation is late Baroque, including the pulpit and altar with a scene of the *Baptism of Jesus Christ*. (P.T.)

Not far from the industrial suburbs of Wałbrzych, in a large park above a steep valley there stands the castle of Książ [150]. It is an enormous edifice, the result of continuous remodelling from a late-13th century Gothic castle of the Świdnica princes through Renaissance and Baroque extensions to its complete rebuilding in the early 20th century. Following wartime devastation, the castle was reconstructed, including the late-Baroque ballroom from the earlier half of the 18th century [151]. (P.T.)

The Thirty Years War was followed by a period of intense building and renewal largely connected with the Counter Reformation. New monastery complexes arose, existing churches received rich, late-Baroque decorations and pilgrim centres were set up. This activity was particularly intense between c. 1690 and 1740. Silesian architects continued to look to Vienna and Prague for their models, a fact clearly reflected in the works of Fischer von Erlach, Hildebrandt and the Dientzenhofers and others. Major but anonymous examples of this architecture include two churches in Krzeszów, a former monastery village whose history is closely connected with the Cistercian abbey [152]. The church of St.Joseph was built in the years 1690–1696 and has a wonderful polychromy by Michael Willmann. The other church is

148. Świdnica. Parish church interiors

149. Świdnica. Protestant Peace church

150. Ksiąz̀. Castle

151. Ksiąz̀. Castle ballroom

the Cistercian church constructed in 1728–1735 on the site of a medieval temple. The latter's richly designed, twin-tower façade with its elegant details reveals an exceptional dynamism that can be compared only with Gothic church architecture. This façade contrasts with the relatively low and modest interiors of the church corpus. The interiors [153], which, however, in their typically late Baroque plan of concave-convex walls of the nave and chapel, as well as broken and repeated pilasters live up to the expectations aroused by the façade. The vaulting was decorated with paintings by Georg Wilhelm Neuhertz, while Ferdinand Brokof and Antonio Dorasil were responsible for the stuccowork and sculptural details. The former Cistercian church in Krzeszów (Grüssau) is a masterpiece of European late-Baroque art.

The temple at Wambierzyce [155], a village at the foot of the Stołowe (Table) Mountains, clearly lacks the artistic qualities of Krzeszów churches. A wide façade at the top of a monumental staircase looks over the site of religious celebrations attracting pilgrims from the surrounding area. The winged, somewhat static façade opens onto a complex interior resembling a labyrinth, with an extended octagonal nave covered with an elliptical cupola. These elements date from the years 1715–1720 when the existing church was considerably enlarged.

The terrace of twelve wooden weavers' houses in Chełmsko Śląskie [153], originating from the early 18th century, is an unusual monument. These arcaded wooden framework houses known as the Twelve Apostles once belonged to a larger group of such buildings. (P.T.)

The health resort of Sokolec [157] offering tourist facilities and excellent winter skiing conditions is situated below the Wielka Sowa, the highest peak in the Sowie (Owl) Mountains, a range belonging to the Central Sudeten, built from Precambrian gneiss, the oldest rock formation in Silesia.

Zagórze Śląskie lies on the northwestern edge of the Sowie Mountains. It is a favoured holiday resort for the inhabitants of such local towns as Wałbrzych and Świdnica, although summer visitors are beginning to come from further away. The village is attractively located on the River Bystrzyca [156], a tributary of the Odra, near the artificial Lake Lubachowski, among steeply sloping and heavily wooded hills. A well-equipped water sports centre has been established on the lake, while the village is another good tourist base for excursions into the nearby mountains. Near Zagórze Śląskie there is a picturesque wooded hill known as

152. Krzeszów. Cistercian abbey

153. Krzeszów. Cistercian church interiors

Chojnica Mountain, on the top of which there are the ruins of Grono Castle, guarding Bystrzyca and environs. This is one of the oldest monuments of architecture in Lower Silesia, raised in the early 14th century by Prince Bolko I of Świdnica. It was enlarged in the 16th century and destroyed during the Thirty Years War. The Gothic and Renaissance walls were adapted in the 19th century during a limited reconstruction. Today the castle houses a regional museum.

The Stołowe Montains are a characteristic group forming part of the Middle Sudeten, built of Tertiary sandstones in two layers, separated from each other and the surroundings by perpendicular rocks. The top layer consists of several isolated, cracked blocks that have undergone weathering and formed labyrinths and interesting rock formations. (I.J.K.)

The Kłodzko Basin is the largest intermontane basin of the Sudeten. The climate is mild and there are valuable mineral springs in many of the towns; all of them are known for their beautiful scenery. Consequently, the Basin is one of the most frequently visited recreational areas in Poland.

Duszniki has functioned as a spa since the turn of the 18th century, although its mineral springs were already referred to in 1408. The settlement developed as an old industrial centre whose inhabitants from the Middle Ages until as late as 1879 earned their living from extracting and smelting iron ore, as well as weaving from the 16th century. In 1562 one of the oldest paper mills in this part of Europe was opened. The wooden mill of 1605 [159] is one of many historic buildings in the town. In August the Frederick Chopin festival is held in Duszniki in commemmoration of the composer's visit in 1826.

Międzygórze [160], situated in a deep sheltered valley of the River Wilczka, is an attractive holiday resort. The first settlement was founded there in the 15th century by woodcutters and charcoal burners. The greatest attraction in the vicinity is the largest waterfall in the Sudeten Mountains (28 m) [161]. (I.J.K.)

Bystrzyca Kłodzka [162], situated on the high left bank of the River Nysa Kłodzka, at its confluence with the River Bystrzyca, grew out of an 11th century Slavic settlement. The town became an important early-industrial centre in the Middle Ages. Its medieval fortified character has survived, including historic buildings going back to the 13th century.

154. Chełmsko Śląskie. Weavers' houses

155. Wambierzyce. Pilgrims' church

Lądek Zdrój is a historic town founded in the 13th century as well as a spa with equally ancient traditions; mention of the healing quality of its waters was first made in 1272, while bathing rooms were set up there in the late 15th century. As with other towns in the Kłodzko Basin, the spa was rapidly developed in the 19th century. Johann Wolfgang Goethe and Ivan Turgenev were among the better-known patients of the sanatorium here. Beautiful Baroque-façaded town houses dating from the 16th and 17th centuries front the Market Place [163]. There is also an old arched stone bridge over the river Biała Lądecka.

The main urban centre in the Basin is Kłodzko [164], one of Silesia's oldest towns, mentioned in chronicles dating from the year 981 as a stronghold on the Polish-Bohemian border; it was first referred to as a "town" in a document dating from 1114. Together with the entire Kłodzko region, it changed hands back and forth between the Poles and Bohemians on various occasions, to become a fief of the Bohemian kings in 1348. In the 16th century it was annexed by Austria, and was taken over by Prussia in the mid-18th century. The town's prosperity was then checked; it became, above all, a strategic location. Kłodzko continued to function as a fortress town until 1877. It retained lively contacts with Poland. In the 14th century the "Florian Psalter", one of the oldest surviving texts in the Polish language, was written here. As late as the 18th century all municipal documents were recorded in Polish. (I.J.K.)

In the Sudeten Forehills, in the central part of the Strzelin massif, on the river Oława, there is Henryków, a settlement founded by prince Henry the Bearded in 1225 next to the Cistercian monastery which he also established. Until the mid-18th century the monastery was an economic and cultural centre for this part of Silesia. In the years 1268–73 (and later, in the 14th century), the Henryków Book was written here; it is an important source of knowledge about medieval Poland, containing descriptions of the economic, social and ethnic conditions in Silesia. The first known sentence written in Polish can be found in the Latin text of the Book. The post-Cistercian monastery complex is a valuable architectural monument.

The Sudeten Foreland is a gently rolling plain, with several isolated massifs built of hard crystalline rock: Ślęża, Strzegom and Strzelin, supplying valu-

156. Zagórze Śląskie. Bystrzyca ravine

157. Sowie Mountains. Mt. Sokolec

158. Stołowe Mountains. Pieskowa Skała (Dog's Head)

159. Kłodzko Basin. Old paper-mill in Duszniki Zdrój

162. Kłodzko Basin.
Bystrzyca Kłodzka

160. Kłodzko Basin. Międzygórze

161. Kłodzko Basin. Waterfall on the
River Wilczka in Międzygórze

163. Kłodzko Basin.
Market Square
in Lądek Zdrój

164. Kłodzko

165. Henryków. Cistercian abbey

able stone for building and road construction. The granite quarry in Strzelin belongs to the largest [166].

Paczków [167], on the River Nysa Kłodzka, is one of the most beautiful old towns in Silesia. Founded upon Flemish law in 1254 by Thomas, Bishop of Wrocław, it was part of the episcopal "state". In 1428 Paczków was taken by the Hussites and used for a time as a stronghold in their ill-fated rebellion. The town flourished in the 16th century as a cloth-producing centre, exporting to Bohemia, Moravia and Austria. When Paczków was annexed by Prussia in the 18th century, cloth production declined. Paczków, "the Silesian Carcasonne", escaped destruction during the Second World War and has retained the layout and character of a typical medieval town, encircled by walls with three town gates and 19 bastions. It is dominated by the Gothic defence church with its massive tower. In the Market Place, amid Renaissance and Baroque town houses, there is an impressive town hall dating from the mid-16th century, remodelled in the first half of the 19th century in the Classical style, with a Renaissance tower. (I.J.K.)

In spite of the horrendous wartime destruction wreaked on Nysa, the parish church of St.Jacob has largely been preserved [168]. It was erected in 1392–1430 by Piotr of Ząbkowice as a great three-aisled temple with adjoining chapels [169]. High brick piers with stone courses shape the view of the nave in a way reminiscent of Italian Gothic churches. The Czech workshop of the Parlers, however, proved more influential. The Nysa temple has been interpreted as a simplified version of St.Barbara's church in Kutna Hora (Bohemia) begun by Peter Parler. The chapels were raised between the buttresses and contain Gothic and Baroque tombs and epitaphs of the Wrocław bishops, to whom the town at one time belonged. (P.T.)

On the borderline between the Silesian Lowlands and Uplands there is the Chełm Ridge, the highest point of which is called Saint Anne's Mount (400 m). A huge amphitheatre was built at its foot, amid the old basalt quarries. The Monument to the Silesian Insurgents, designed by the modernist Polish sculptor Xawery Dunikowski, stands on top of St.Anne commemorating the Silesian insurgents who fought for Silesia's reunification with Poland [170]. Opole on the Oder [171] was the old centre of the Opolanie tribe. In the 10th century it was a stronghold, becoming

166. Strzelin. Granite quarry

167. Paczków ▷

168. Nysa. St. Jacob church ▷

169. Nysa. St. Jacob church interiors ▷

the seat of a castellanship during the reign of Bolesław the Brave. In 1202 it became the capital of a separate duchy. In 1532 Opole passed to the Habsburgs; it came under the sovereignty of Poland between 1645 and 1666, to be seized by Prussia in 1741. It remained under German rule until 1945. Trade and the crafts flourished under the Piast princes, while under Prussian rule the town became an important industrial centre. Despite the influx of Germans and the pressure of Germanisation policies, Opole was still a strong centre of Polish life. Badly damaged during World War II, it had to be extensively reconstructed, particularly the historic center. Opole possesses numerous church and public buildings of historic interest. Folk dress is also proof of tradition [172].

The town of Brzeg is on the high Oder river bank on the eastern fringe of the Wrocław Plain. There was already a stronghold here in the 11th century, around which a settlement developed. Brzeg was granted municipal rights in 1243 and was the capital of the independent Duchy of Brzeg and Legnica from 1311 to 1675. Brzeg's most prosperous period was in the 16th and 17th centuries, when it produced woollen cloth and Gobelin tapestries. It was in this period that many Renaissance buildings were erected, including the castle of the Brzeg princes (13th–14th centuries), which was later reconstructed leaving very little of the original structure. The two-storey façade of the surviving castle gatehouse [173] is adorned with figures of Silesian princes and also coats-of-arms and plaques, as well as a genealogical tree of the Piast dynasty. (I.J.K.)

Situated in the very heart of the Silesian Lowlands, Wrocław [174] is one of the oldest towns in Poland and for ten centuries has been the main urban centre of Silesia. It developed on the site of an ancient settlement dating back to Neolithic times. At the beginning of its history, Wrocław was a settlement of the Ślężanie tribe. It had most certainly been incorporated into the Polish state by the year 990. It must have played an important role even then, judging by the fact that Bolesław the Brave in 1000 founded here one of the three episcopates subject to the Gniezno metropolitan see. The oldest settlement developed on the islets between the branches of the Oder. The 11th century seat of the princes and bishops was on Tum Islet (Ostrów Tumski). Situated at the intersection of important trade routes, Wrocław developed rapidly. Tum Islet and Piasek Islet became too

◁ 170. Mt. St. Anne. Insurgents Monument

◁ 171. Opole

◁ 172. Opole. Folk costumes

173. Brzeg. Facade of the Castle Gate

174. Wrocław. Old Town

175. Wrocław. Cathedral ▷

176. Wrocław. Town hall ▷

small for the expanding town which moved out onto the river's left bank at the turn of the 12th century. After the death of the last Wrocław Piast prince in 1335, the town was incorporated into Bohemia. It was already one of the largest towns in Central Europe. In the mid-14th century it joined the Hanseatic League. Many Gothic churches and public edifices were raised, more often than not on the sites of existing buildings. The church of the Virgin Mary on Piasek Islet has Gothic interiors characteristic of Wrocław [177] and the Holy Cross church (1288–1350), one of the most valuable Gothic buildings in Poland, used to contain the tomb of it founder [179] Prince Henry IV Probus, now in the National Museum. In 1526 Wrocław came under the rule of the Habsburgs. In the 16th to 18th centuries it enjoyed a long period of economic growth, when many Renaissance and Baroque buildings were erected. In 1741 Wrocław was occupied by the Prussians. In spite of Germanisation policies, the city remained an active centre of Polish culture for a long time. In the interwar period those Poles that were left were still engaged in lively social and cultural activity, which continued even in Hitler's time, despite the repressive measures taken by the authorities. The final battles of the Second World War brought appalling destruction to the city. Reconstructed Wrocław has become an important industrial city, as well as a vital academic and cultural centre. Together with Cracow and Poznań, Wrocław is one of the three major provincial capitals of Poland. (I.J.K.)

The church of St.Cross on Tum Islet was built in 1288 by Prince Henryk IV Probus. Construction was completed in 1350. The two-storey hall church on a cruciforn plan is one of the few churches of the type in Europe.
The presbytery of the St.John the Baptist cathedral in Wrocław [175], originating from the years 1244–1272 is widely recognised as the first Gothic construction in Poland and a model for the cathedral on Cracow's Wawel Hill. The nave was raised in the first half of the 14th century and the twin towers were completed in the 16th century. The cathedral was completely gutted during the siege in 1945, but has been carefully reconstructed. Two Baroque chapels miraculously escaped the fire: St.Elisabeth's (Jacopo Scianzi 1680–1686) and the Electoral Chapel (Hans B.Fischer von Erlach, a Viennese architect, 1715–1724, with polychromy and stucco executed by Italian artists).
Wrocław's town hall [176], as was the case with many medieval municipal

177. Wrocław. St. Mary church in Piaski interiors

178. Wrocław. St. Cross church

179. Wrocław. Prince Henry IV Probus' tomb

180. Wrocław. University viewed from ▷ the Oder river

181. Wrocław. Aula Leopoldina at the ▷ University

edifices, evolved from the combining of a series of town buildings into a single, harmonious complex. The earlier, independent buildings were adapted into a single, effective whole with a rich sculptural program at the end of the 15th century. The project was directed by Hans Berthold, while the team of sculptors included Paul Preusse, a colleague of the famous Arnold of Westphalia. The interiors house a permanent exhibition of the city's history and of the collections of the Medallion Art Museum. (P.T.)

At the turn of the 17th century Silesia witnessed a significant architectural revival inspired by the Jesuits and other religious orders. Wrocław, until that point an overwhelmingly Gothic city, saw the implementation of a rich Baroque program. The Jesuit Collegium and crusaders' monastery were raised along the Oder embankment. By this time, Baroque was in its late phase, reflected in the dynamic qualities of external mass and picturesque interior effects, lavishly decorated with sculptures and wall paintings. The Jesuit Collegium was begun around 1728. The University has been quartered in this impressive building since 1811 [180]. This edifice has been tentatively attributed to Johann Martinelli. The assembly hall [181] with an illusionist painting depicting the *Apotheosis of Divine Wisdom* in the vaulting is a good illustration of late-Baroque interior art. (P.T.)

The other Baroque façade reflected in the Oder waters is the former Red Star Crusaders monastery built in 1675–1715. Its plan is that of a three-winged palace adjoining a lower, riverside building under a cupola. The French architect Jean-Baptiste Mathieu was probably responsible for this building; he was presumably also the author of the Prague temple belonging to the same order. It is a more compact edifice revealing a stronger Classical bias than any other Baroque building in Eastern and Central Europe. The Ossoliński National Foundation, an important Polish cultural institution founded in 1817 in Lvov, has been housed in the former monastery since 1945 [182]. Important historic writings are kept here, and the Institute's publishing house is located here as well. In addition, the Ossolineum owns prints, numismatic and medal collections. (P.T.)

Among Wrocław's twelve museums, the National Museum has the largest collections. It was inaugurated in 1947 in a devastated city whose museum treasures had been reduced to a fraction of their former greatness. Part of the present Wrocław collections originates from the pre-war museums of Lvov. Permanent exhibitions of Silesian medieval art are of unique value as are the Baroque sculptures. The National Mu-

182. Wrocław. Ossolineum Institute seen from the river

183. Oleśnica. Castle

184. Trzebnica. Post-Cistercian
church, tympanum with King David

185. The Oder river valley. Marsh meadow woods

187. Legnica. Gate leading to the castle

188. Żagań. Palace

186. Legnickie Pole. Church interior

seum also possesses a valuable collection of 19th century and contemporary Polish art. Silesian ceramics and glass, for centuries manufactured in the province, are also well represented. The only section devoted to the art of book binding and historic publication in Poland is also be found here.

The rich collections of the Ossolineum as well as the medal collection in the Town Hall, going back to the 16th century, have already been mentioned. The Archdiocese Museum also contains a rich collection of Silesian Gothic art, part of which is permanently exhibited in the Virgin Mary church on Piasek Islet. Wrocław possesses the only Museum of Architecture in Poland, housed in historic monastery and church buildings from the 15th and 16th centuries. (P.T.)

To the northeast of Wrocław there is the town of Oleśnica. In the 11th century, on the site of today's town, there was a princely stronghold and trading settlement situated on a trade route running from Wrocław to Wielkopolska. In 1240, the Piast prince Henry II of Wrocław founded a castle on the site of the Slavic settlement. The castle was rebuilt in the 16th century as a Renaissance palace [183]. In 1312, as a result of feudal divisions, a separate Duchy of Oleśnica was created. After the death of the last Piast prince in 1492, Oleśnica passed into the hands of the Bohemian Podiebrads, and then, in 1647, the Würtenberg princes. In the 16th century, Oleśnica was a vital centre of the Polish Protestant movement. In the 18th century cotton-spinning developed here, and with the Age of Steam factory industries. The town was largely destroyed during the last war. It has been rebuilt as an industrial centre with tourist facilities. (I.J.K.)

Trzebnica, situated among hills, was once a tribal centre. As a market settlement it received municipal status in the mid 13th century. In 1207 Henry the Bearded and his wife Hedvig founded and richly equipped the first Cistercian convent in Silesia. From that time on, the history of the town and the abbey were closely linked, Trzebnica becoming the centre of economic life. In the 16th–18th centuries, the spinning of linen was developed here, and woolen cloth weaving in the 18th century. A spa with its own mineral water springs opened at the close of the 19th century is still in operation. Trzebnica was badly damaged in the Second World War, but the abbey complex has survived along with a 13th century Gothic church. It has beautiful Romanesque portals [184] with sculptures in the tympanums.

Extensive marshland forests at one time stretched along the wide Oder plain [185]. They survive in smaller enclaves to this day in the vicinities of Racibórz, Koźle, Oława, Wrocław, Wołowa and Środa Śląska. (I.J.K.)

The church in Legnickie Pole is one of the most beautiful late-Baroque buildings in Poland. It was designed in 1727–1731 by Kilian Ignatz Dientzenhofer, the architect of many magnificent Prague churches, such as St.Michael's in the Old Town and the Ursuline Sisters in the Hradčany. Dientzenhofer sought new spatial solutions, introducing with relish a plan consisting of interconnecting circles and ellipses to lend the interiors a unique, dynamic fluidity. This plan was used in the new church of St.Hedvig [186] built for the Czech Benedictines on the site of a great and victorious battle with the Tartars in 1241 during which the Silesian prince Henry the Pious lost his life. Vaclav Reiner, another Prague artist, was responsible for the paintings, while those adorning the altar were the work of Francisco Backer from Antwerp. The magnificent polychromy was executed by Cosmo Damian Asm of Munich in 1733. (P.T.)

The Cistercian monastery at Lubiąż from the years 1690–1720 [189] was one of the great religious complexes raised in Silesia during the Counter Reformation. The church, incorporated into a grandiose façade stretching virtually one quarter of a kilometre, conceals Gothic walls originating from the early 14th century. A splendid library with polychromy by Christian F.Bentum has been preserved in the monastery, as well as the prince's hall from 1734–1738, containing richly painted and sculptured decoration designed to glorify the Habsburg dynasty. (P.T.)

189. Lubiąż. Cistercian abbey

Wielkopolska Lowland

191. Biskupin. Peninsula

◁ 190. Lowland landscape

The Wielkopolska Lowlands are the cradle of the Polish state. It was here that the oldest fortified settlements of the Polanie tribe developed in the 8th and 9th centuries. This was the nucleus of the Polish state. It is an area of very old settlements, dating back to the Neolithic Age. Among the vestiges of the old settlers, Biskupin is a site of international importance. It is a fortified settlement from the times of the Lusatian culture in the early Iron Age (about 550 B C), and was discovered in 1933 on a former island, today a peninsula on Lake Biskupin, near Żnin [191]. Excavations revealed the ground plan of the settlement, while tools, and other objects found there enabled scholars to reconstruct the life of its inhabitants. The settlement had a population of about 1,000. The main occupations were agriculture and husbandry. The remains of artisan workshops have also been found. On the basis of these archeological finds, several houses and parts of the defence rampart and breakwater have been reconstructed [192]. (I.J.K.)

One of the places associated with the creation of the Polish state is Ostrów Lednicki, an island on Lake Lednica [193] with traces of a settlement dating from the Mesolithic period. At the turn of the 9th century, a third of the island was taken up by a stronghold surrounded by high ramparts. Inside the stronghold there are the remains of a stone palatium. According to tradition, Bolesław the Brave, the first crowned King of Poland, was born at Ostrów Lednicki.

Gniezno was the first capital of the Polish state united by Mieszko I [194]. Its name is derived from the Polish word *gniazdo* (nest) and is associated with the legend about an eagle's nest found by Lech, the legendary ancestor of the Poles. In the year 1000, the emperor Otto III visited Gniezno as a pilgrim to the tomb of the bishop Wojciech (Adalbert), who lost his life during a mission in Borussia and was canonized soon after. He was sumptuously received by Bolesław the Brave. The Gniezno Archbishopric and metropolitan see were founded them. In 1025 Bolesław the Brave was crowned there. The political role of Gniezno diminished after the devastation of the town during the invasion of Bretislav of Bohemia in 1039. But it still remained – and has until today – the historic seat of Church authorities in Poland.

The Old Town quarter has retained its urban layout and many of the old buildings. The oldest of them, a pre-Romanesque church, was burnt down in 1018. A Romanesque church was erected in its place by Bolesław the Brave. A Gothic cathedral [194, 196], was raised on its foundations in the

192. Biskupin. Defence walls and gate (reconstructed)

193. Ostrów Lednicki.

years 1342–1372, and in the 17th and 18th centuries it was remodelled and surrounded by a wreath of Renaissance and Baroque chapels. This cathedral was burnt down in 1945. It has been rebuilt in its old form. The most valuable relics in the cathedral are the Romanesque bronze doors (about 1170) covered with reliefs showing scenes from the life and death of St. Adalbert [195]. (I.J.K.)

Poznań is the chief city of the Wielkopolska Lowlands. It is situated in the valley of the River Warta at a place where the river can be crossed conveniently. As early as the 9th century, between the Warta and its tributary, the Cybina, on the island that came to be known as Ostrów Tumski (Tum Islet) [197], there was a stronghold, under the protection of which a settlement developed. The city's mythical founder was called Poznań. In the mid-10th century, this stronghold was enlarged and made into a powerful fortress sharing the functions of the state capital with Gniezno, accommodating the favourite princely residence and from 968 Poland's first episcopal seat. Poznań was destroyed by Prince Bretislav of Bohemia. During the period of feudal divisions operated as the capital of the Wielkopolska line of the Piast dynasty. The town began to expand. A settlement arose on the Cybina's right bank, known as Śródka, which in 1230 was granted municipal status. However, neither Śródka nor Ostrów Tumski could accommodate the town's rapid growth, and prince Przemysław I of Wielkopolska transferred its economic centre to the Warta's left bank. In 1253 left-bank Poznań received its charter in accordance with Magdeburg Law. A castle was raised there at the end of the 13th century. Defence walls were built around the town, which also received a Gothic town hall at the turn of the 13th century. Granted numerous privileges, Poznań developed rapidly, outpacing Gniezno to become the main urban centre of Wielkopolska. A trade route from Mazovia, Lithuania and the Old Ruthenian territories to Leipzig as well as from Cracow to Szczecin passed through Poznań. The city experienced its golden era in the 16th and 17th centuries. It also had a well developed network of handicraft workshops and was a centre of the medical sciences. The town was expanded and many alterations and additions carried out. Printing and bookbinding evolved. Poznań became an important cultural and educational centre; in 1519 bishop Lubrański founded an academy there. The Reformation greatly influenced the city at this time. The town expanded; new suburbs arose and many public buildings were constructed, including mansions and palaces for the noble families. (I.J.K.)

196. Gniezno. Cathedral interiors

194. Gniezno

195. Gniezno. Cathedral and part
    of the doors

168

In connection with Poland's adoption of Christianity in 966, the construction of a monumental cathedral was commenced on Ostrów Tumski islet. Its remnants have survived in the vaults of the present temple. This first cathedral was connected with the imperial foundations and its form was similar to Benedictine churches raised in the West. A new, Romanesque cathedral was constructed in 1058–1079, and then a Gothic one in 1346–1428. The latter was related to Pomeranian and Silesian Gothic, although in some elements it resembled the French cathedrals [198]. The choir, as in western cathedrals, received an ambulatory which was assured additional lighting by the placing of lights above three of the ambulatory bays of the great tower. They completely altered the eastern elevation. The ambulatory opens onto three chapels, the centrally positioned one was adapted at a later date into the Golden Chapel [199].

This chapel received a Romantic-Byzantine decor in the years 1815–1840 in an attempt to commemorate Mieszko I and Bolesław the Brave buried in the cathedral. Designed by the architect Francesco M. Lanci and the sculptor Christian Rauch, the chapel's construction was funded from resources donated by the people of Wielkopolska. It reflects a carefully conceived historic and national program aimed at creating a patriotic sanctuary for the Poles living under Prussian authority after the partitions. The chapel's form was intended to refer to the pre-Romanesque rotunda church at Ostrów Lednicki which at that time was being researched and had come to be considered as one of the first Piast palatia. The Byzantine style at this time was regarded as the art form most suitably reflecting the era of Piast Poland. "The Creator of the Universe" surrounded by the holy apostles, emblems of various illustrious Polish families and bishops adorn the chapel interiors and were intended to express a conviction that Old Poland had arisen under holy and spiritual direction. A copy of Titian's *Assuna* placed in the altar had the opening words of an old Polish knights' hymn "The Holy Virgin Mother" added. Paintings portray Mieszko I refuting the pagan gods and Otto III with Bolesław the Brave at St.Adalbert's grave. The figure of Bolesław the Brave was given the facial features of a contemporary hero, Prince Józef Poniatowski. The Golden Chapel exemplifies a work of art conceived in line with a national ideology for a society which had been deprived of its independence. (P.T.)

197. Poznań. Ostrów Tumski.

198. Poznań. Cathedral interiors

The old, Gothic town hall in the Market Square [200] first received its arcades in 1508 before undergoing fundamental rebuilding in 1550–1560 in the Renaissance style, together with beautifully executed interior decoration [201]. The loggia was completed with parapet walls, while the façade received scratchwork and polychrome details. A Neo-Classical tower was added in 1781–1783. The Gothic-Renaissance town houses standing next to the town hall also date from the 15th–17th centuries, as well as many of those fronting the Market Square which were later redesigned in the Baroque or Neo-Classical styles.

Following its decline in the 17th century, Poznań began to recover in the age of the Enlightenment, when trading was revived and manufacturing activities developed (mainly textile mills). Following the Second Partition (1793), Poznań fell under Prussian rule, although for a while it did get a reprieve as capital of the Grand Duchy of Poznań, autonomous until 1848. In the second quarter of the 19th century Poznań became an important scientific and cultural centre. In 1829 Edward Raczyński founded a library [202] and in the ensuing years publishing and printing houses along with bookshops and libraries were opened. In 1857 the Poznań Society of the Friends of Science was set up. In spite of Germanisation policies, Polish society always acted in solidarity. This was a period of economic growth for the city; apart from providing services for the agrarian populace of Wielkopolska, it also served expanded trading. After the secularisation of Church property in 1797, church property and private townships were incorporated into the town. However, town planning possibilities were to be severely limited by the Prussian citadel and its system of fortifications which were raised in 1829–39; the defence walls at least were removed in 1900 leading to massive and rapid urban development. The First World War raised hopes of regaining independence. The Wielkopolska Uprising broke out on 27th December, 1918; within a few days Poznań had been liberated. Despite industrial development, the city's trade functions continued to prevail throughout the interwar years. The Poznań Fair was organised in 1921, in keeping with the medieval traditions of the St.John Fairs. The Poznań Fair assumed an international character after 1925 and has continued to take place annually in peacetime ever since. In 1939 Poznań and Wielkopolska were incorporated into the Nazi Reich. The incorporation was inevitably accompanied by arrests, deportations and destruction of Polish national monuments. Liberation from German occupation brought considerable destru-

199. Poznań. Cathedral, the Golden Chapel interior

200. Poznań. Market Square

ction to the city, especially the city centre. Reputed for their organisational talents and industrious nature, the inhabitants of Poznań rebuilt their city rapidly. A new central district was designed and new residential complexes sprung up. New schools of higher education were opened. Cultural and artistic life has been very active. The Poznań Polish Theatre has achieved wide renown, while the opera house and philharmonic belong to the country's very best. The Choir of the State Philharmonic has won international acclaim. The destroyed or dilapidated historic buildings have been restored, a number to their historic appearance lost during the 19th century. They are largely concentrated in the Old Town and Ostrów Tumski preserving the medieval street layout. Poznań attracts a fair number of tourists. (I.J.K.)

The Post-Jesuit church was constructed over a long period. Begun in the years 1649–1653, it was not completed until 1732. A whole pleiad of monk architects worked on the complex under the direction of Bartłomiej Wąsowski. Most of these were Italians, and Wąsowski himself had visited Italy. The overall project was inevitably orientated to the temples of Rome, offering another exceptionally rich program of interior decoration [203], a superb synthesis of architecture, painting and sculpture. Massive, deep red columns resembling a theatre backdrop direct the visitor's eye towards a modestly lit altar. In spite of the long period of construction, the overall effect is remarkably consistent, evoking powerful images of pathos and monumentality. (P.T.)

Museums in Poznań possess rich and interesting collections. The National Muzeum in Poznań dates back to 1857 and its collections include numerous excellent examples of Polish art ranging from the Middle Ages to modern times. There are also valuable European paintings, especially from the 16th century Italian and 17th century Dutch schools, as well as Poland's most valuable collection of Spanish paintings. European decorative arts are exhibited separately. The Museum also possesses divisions in Rogalin, Gołuchów and Śmiełów palaces. (P.T.)

Rogalin is located 17 km south of Poznań on the banks of the Warta, formerly a knightly dominion. From the 18th century until the Second World War Rogalin belonged to the Raczyński family who were widely-known patrons of the arts. Their former palace in the Baroque and Classicistic styles [204] dating from the period 1770–1782 and joined to its outbuildings by two galleries, possesses beautiful Classicistic interiors, including

201. Poznań. Town hall loggia

202. Poznań. Raczyński Library

203. Poznań. Post-Jesuit church interiors

204. Rogalin. Raczyński palace

205. Rogalin oaks

the drawing room and groundfloor which were designed by Domenico Merlini, and a staircase made by Johann C. Kamsetzer. Separate rooms were constructed in 1909–10 to house a collection of Polish and European paintings from the 19th and early 20th centuries. The palace was plundered by the Nazis in the last war. The palace's main corpus at present houses a division of the National Museum in Poznań. Apart from a permanent exhibition of palace interiors from the 17th–19th centuries, the building houses a collection of paintings originally belonging to Edward Raczyński. The palace stands in a gorgeous park laid out in the 18th century, partly in the French and partly in the English style. There is a mausoleum-chapel of the Raczyński family situated in the park and dating back to 1820. It is a copy of the Roman temple in Nimes. The park includes the largest complex of ancient and enormous oaks in Poland (954 in all, up to 9 m in diameter) [205].

The town of Kórnik, situated to the southeast of Poznań, owes its fame to the museum and library founded in 1839 by Tytus Działyński; they are housed in a castle dating from the 16th century (on the site of a yet older, wooden castle from 1426). The castle was raised for the owners of Kórnik, the Górka family, and rebuilt in the years 1845–60 in the Romantic Gothic style [206]. The museum contains a priceless collection of church and secular art, archeological findings as well as natural science exhibits from Poland and other countries [207]. The library, containing in excess of 150,000 volumes and a collection of Polish prints from the 16th–18th centuries, belongs to the Polish Academy of Sciences. The castle's last owner, Władysław Zamoyski, presented the castle and library with the estate as a gift to the Polish nation. The castle is surrounded by a park originally laid out during the 16th century in the Italian style, later converted into the French style to be finally redesigned in the English-Romantic style of the early 19th century. Today it contains the largest dendrological park originating from the research carried out by Działyński and his son, Jan Kanty. (I.J.K.)

The surrounding countryside of Lake Gopło, Wielkopolska'a largest lake, abounds in legends and myths telling of the origins of the Polish state. The angels are supposed to have visited the wheelwright Piast, a myth possibly inspired by the biblical visit of Abraham. The legend also tells of the hated Prince Popiel who was devoured by mice in his tower. Although the Mouse Tower [208] was in reality part of a castle built by Casimir the Great in the 14th century, archeologists have discovered the

206. Kórnik. Castle

207. Kórnik. Moorish room
in the castle

174

remains of an earlier settlement on the
site. The lake today stretches for about
25 km, whereas in the 2nd century AD
when the Roman amber trail operated,
it extended at least 40 km. The Romans
knew of Kruszwica as a settlement,
which in the 8th–9th centuries evolved
into a defensive stronghold. The
three-aisled Romanesque collegiate
church [209] from 1120–40 is the town's
most treasured historic monument. The
eastern end is particularly harmonious
and terminates in five semicircular
apses linking the collegiate church with
the temples characteristic of western
Europe.
An exceptional work of Romanesque
architecture has been preserved in
Strzelno. It is the rotunda of St.Prokop
[210] from the later part of the 12th
century with interesting interiors next
to the church of St.Trinity and a monastery belonging to the Norbertan
Nuns; the walls between the aisles are
surmounted on Romanesque columns
[211] uncovered when the Baroque fac-
ings were removed in 1946. The shafts
of two such columns are decorated with
figural sculptures. Figures in the arcades symbolise human virtues and
defects in line with medieval moral
treatises. This type of artistic rendering
is unique in European art. Other examples of Romanesque sculpture have
also survived in the church and reflect
its former splendour. (P.T.)

The church in Inowrocław was originally raised at the end of the 12th
century. A single nave with two towers
suggests a more complex design. The
façade is composed of granite blocks
adorned with stone-carved masks [212]
which must have been associated with
some mystical function. (P.T.)

Salt has represented an important natural resource in Kujawy for centuries. It
was washed out of underground salt
domes for the first time in the late 18th
century, while in 1822–28 two twin
graduation towers were built in Ciechocinek for the purposes of the spa. In
1859 a third such tower was raised
[213]. Ciechocinek has become a large
health resort with baths, pump rooms
and sanatoria erected among beautifully kept parks. (I.J.K.)

Bydgoszcz has its origins in a fortified
settlement founded in the days of Bolesław the Brave to guard the dry passage
through the swampy old valley of the
Vistula. The town developed rapidly
from the 15th century on and became
an important centre trading in wheat,
timber and salt until the mid-17th century. A reminder of those days are the
large granaries and salt warehouses of
1874 and the 19th century [214]. Germanisation was particularly strong

208. Lake Gopło and the Mouse
     Tower

209. Kruszwica. Collegiate church

210. Strzelno. St. Procopius rotunda church

211. Strzelno. Detail of the columns in the Norbertan Nuns church

here. Steps were taken to destroy historical buildings attesting to the town's Polish character; the castle, some ancient churches and monasteries and even secular buildings were pulled down. The town's expansion in the 1930s was halted by the Second World War; the German occupation began with mass executions and a deportation of a considerable part of the town's population. Bydgoszcz has developed greatly after the war and has become a major administrative, cultural and academic centre. (I.J.K.)

The Łagów lake region is an attractive tourist area. Lake Łagów is perhaps the most beautiful [215] with its high embankments, ravines and deciduous woods. It is linked with the larger and also charming Lake Ciecz. The town of Łagów is situated on an isthmus between the two lakes in a long glacial spillway. An ancient stronghold there was seized by Brandenburg in the mid-13th century. In the years 1299–1346, it was a knights' fief and thereafter, until 1810, it belonged to the Knights of St.John of Jerusalem, who built a great castle with a 35 m high tower in the early 14th century [216]. This castle was seriously damaged during the last war, but following Łagów's reincorporation into Poland it was rebuilt and adapted to serve as a hotel. (I.J.K.)

Zielona Góra [217] lies in a basin amid morraine hills composing the Zielona Góra elevation. The town was most probably founded in the second half of the 13th century and was granted municipal status in 1323. It belonged to the Silesian Piast line of Głogów – Żagań until 1488. The rulers were subject to the Bohemian Crown until the mid-14th century, and to Hungaria – in the 15th century. The town developed in the 15th and 16th centuries thanks to the cloth and wine industries, introduced in the 13th century. The production of wine declined in the 18th century never to recover, although even today a small number of vineyards ensures wine production on a limited scale. The annual Vintage Festival draws tourists from all over the country. Cloth production was industrialised in the 19th century. Other branches of industry also developed, including metallurgy and machine production. Upon returning to Poland after the Second World War, Zielona Góra gained favourable conditions to develop as an industrial and cultural centre and voivodship capital. (I.J.K.)

212. Inowrocław. St. Mary Church, masks on the church walls

213. Ciechocinek. Wooden gradation towers

214. Bydgoszcz. Warehouses on the Brda river

215. The Łagów Lakeland. Łagów lake

Some interesting vestiges of timber architecture can be found in Wielkopolska. Rakoniewice, a small town and market centre in the Poznań lake district possesses the richest collection of wooden buildings, including some 18th century houses with arcades [218] once belonging to the town's craftsmen. Rakoniewice had a developed crafts and trade economy prior to its incorporation in 1772 into Prussia. The nearby town of Buk has an interesting 18th century Baroque cemetery and a church of the Holly Cross [219].

Leszno is located in the historical Wschowa land which formed a border zone between Wielkopolska and Silesia. The princes of both provinces claimed the area until in 1343 Casimir the Great succeeded in making it part of Wielkopolska. At the turn of the 14th century, the Wschowa land belonged to the Wieniawita knights who adopted the name of Leszczyński from the settlement. The town was granted municipal status in 1547. In the mid-16th century, it became a centre of the Reformation. Rafał Leszczyński, a sympathizer of the movement, brought the Bohemian Brethren here. A Lutheran community was also established in Leszno in 1633. The Bohemian Brethren's elementary school was founded in 1555 and was then turned into a secondary school. Its rector was Jan Amos Komensky, a Bohemian pedagogue and writer who had fled from persecution. Leszno became at this time a significant cultural and publishing centre. Tragedy hit Leszno after the Swedish invasions when Polish troops burned the town in revenge for its support of the enemy and exiled the Bohemian Brethren. From the early 18th century Leszno belonged to Stanisław Leszczyński who, twice elected king of Poland, was himself forced into exile by the Russians. In 1738 Leszno was purchased by the Sułkowski family. In 1797, in connection with Poland's Second Partition, the town was incorporated into Prussia. Between the world wars, Leszno was a thriving economic centre in the southern part of Wielkopolska and has continued to develop as such until the present day. Although destroyed many times, the town has retained its medieval layout and a number of buildings of historical interest, crowned by the magnificent Baroque town hall [220] which after a fire was rebuilt under the guidance of Pompeo Ferrari at the beginning of the 18th century. (I.J.K.)

The small and old town of Osieczna lies 10 km northeast of Leszno, on Lake Łoniewskie. It is regional crafts and market centre, but also a spa with its own baths. Osieczna has a number of historic monuments, the most highly prized of which include three wooden windmills from the later half of the 18th

216. Łagów. Knights of Jerusalem castle

217. Zielona Góra. City centre

century [221]. Also situated near Leszno, Radyna is a small historic town with Baroque layout. Its main axis is a street linking the market place with the palace of the former owners. The town is known for the Baroque residence of the Leszczyński family [222], erected in 1685–95 on Gothic foundations of a 15th century castle belonging to the Rydzyński family. The west wing of the palace was built by Pompeo Ferrari in 1700 and was burned down during the Northern War. August Sułkowski, the successive owner, had the architect Frantz rebuild the palace in 1742–45. The first storey was extended to form a rectangle enclosing a central courtyard. A large park on a geometrical plan was laid out in the 17th century. In 1762 Sułkowski, founded a Piarist Academy in Rydzyna. He expressed the wish that in the event of his family dying out, the whole estate would be devoted to educational purposes. The wish had to wait until Poland's rebirth in the 20th century before it could be fulfilled. Following the death of the last Sułkowski, the Rydzyna estate was seized by the Prussian authorities. It was only in 1928 that the "Sułkowski Foundation" set up a secondary school with dormitories in the palace. After a fire in 1945, the palace was rebuilt. (I.J.K.)

In Gołuchów there is a romantic castle [223] raised after 1872 as a museum in an enormous landscape park with many exotic trees. Originally, a defensive manor house dating from c.1560 stood on the site; it was rebuilt in the early 17th century as a magnificent palace by the voivode Wacław Leszczyński. By the 19th century the palace had become a ruin which was adapted by its then owners, Jan Działyński and his wife, Izabella of the Czartoryskis, to house their art collections, including priceless ancient vases. The building was the work of French artists, whereas the sculptural decoration consisted largely of 16th century objects from the ruins of demolished French and Italian monuments. The courtyard walls were covered with fragments of bas-reliefs, mosaics and medallions. Following destruction in the last war, when the art collections were dispersed, the castle was acquired by the National Museum in Poznań. A series of stylistic interiors [224] has survived, as well as a number of hearths and portals with the date of 1619 which belonged to the palace of the Leszczyński.

When Zofia of the Opaliński family visited Venice in 1676, she was so greatly inspired by Baldassare Longhena's church of Santa Maria della Salute that on returning to Gostyń she requested that the Italian architect Giorgio Catenaci recreate Longhena's masterpiece. The nave, based on a similar octagonal plan, was built in 1679–1698.

218. Rakoniewice. Arcaded wooden houses

219. Buk. Cemetery church of the Holy Cross

Pompeo Ferrari completed the construction in 1726–1728, raising the dome on a huge drum and closing the presbytery. Ferrari was responsible for severa architectural projects in Wielkopolska. He married and settled down in Poland. He died in 1736 in Rydzyna. The interior decoration of the dome, as that at Ląd, was executed by the famous Silesian painter Georg W. Neunhertz. This artist was also responsible for the eight scenes painted on the dome, depicting the life of St. Philip, patron of the Philipine Order for whom the church was raised. The frescoes impress with their freedom of composition, the sweeping pictorial treatment and full lively colours. (P.T.)

In the late 16th and first half of the 17th century, the Polish gentry built stone manor houses combining the Italian mannerist style with local, traditional forms. One such example can be found in Poddębice [229]. It belonged to Zygmunt Grudziński, voivode of Rawa. It was erected in 1610–1617. The freely composed façade consists of a tower, staircase and two-level loggias with flat-topped arches. A triangular gable above the cornice is richly decorated with pinnacles. The gable, as much as the stuccoed decoration of the loggia vaulting, is particularly typical of Polish mannerism. (P.T.)

Kalisz [228] is among Poland's oldest towns; it was mentioned in the 2nd century AD by the Roman geographer Ptolemy as an important stop on the amber trail. Kalisz prospered in the 16th and 17th centuries as a linen manufacturing centre. The Jesuits built one of their first churches in Poland (1587–1595). Most of the official buildings, however, date from the early 19th century and were designed by Sylwester Szpilowski. (P.T.)

One of the very best preserved wooden manor houses dating from 1757 can be found in Ożarów [230]. The manor house as the residence of the Polish gentry played a significant role in the history and culture of Poland. The tradition endured into the 20th century. The manor house consisted of a main building on a rectangular plan with alcove chambers in the corners, following in this the 17th-century stone residences erected in the Vasa period. The building's characteristic form is emphasised by a mansard roof, which is referred to as a Polish roof. It is always shingled. The main entrance tended to be in the form of a porch with columns. (P.T.)

Wooden churches in Old Poland were often painted on the inside. An interesting example of polychrome decoration can be admired in the beamed ceiling at Grębień [225]. The church was raised around 1500; its interior decoration is

220. Leszno. Town hall

221. Osieczna. Windmills

222. Rydzyna. Leszczyński palace

some 20 years later. The exuberant floral patterns, borrowed from Renaissance prints, are at variance with traditional motifs and transform the ceiling into a heavenly garden. The characters of musicians – courtly with the lute, rural with the fiddle – are also depicted here. (P.T.)

Although granted municipal status in 1423, Łódź [231] is a 19th century urban phenomenon. Widescale industrialisation launched by the government of the Polish Kingdom, created at the Congress of Vienna as an autonomous part of the Russian Empire, anticipated the rapid development of the textile industry in a large, undeveloped area between the Vistula and Warta rivers with its abundant natural water supply. Numerous settlements were founded in this watershed, attracting settlers from Bohemia, Saxony and Silesia. Łódź grew into a leading settlement in this industrial area. In the years 1835–1837, Ludwik Geyer built Poland's first steam spinning mill here. Other industrialists followed his example. The lifting of customs barriers between the Congress Kingdom and Russia in 1850 opened up vast markets for the Łódź industries: more and more factories were built while production became increasingly specialised. This boom coincided with the building of the railway. During the 1914–1918 war, machines and installations were removed on a huge scale in consequence of the German effort to „de-industrialize" the area. Łódź recovered to some extent after 1918, although the loss of its Russian markets as well as the Great Depression of the early-1930s seriously hampered further growth. Annexed to the Third Reich in 1939, Łódź endured over five years of persecutions. Following liberation, the town's industrial works which had not been destroyed, restarted their production quickly. Later years brought a degree of modernisation to the textile industry, while the chemical, engineering and clothing industries as well as other factories were expanded. The town has become an important cultural centre, the seat of a university and other higher schools of learning, with theatres, a philharmonic, museums and numerous libraries. Łódź is Poland's second most populous city after Warsaw.

The territorial development of Łódź initially followed the plans of R.Rembieliński, i.e., in a southerly direction from the original little town. At this time the Nowe Miasto, or New Town, was laid out with Plac Wolności (Freedom Square) at its centre [232], fronted by the town hall and a Protestant church. The town continued to develop southwards along the axis of the main Piotrowska Street [233]. The town's development was intended to follow a rational plan regarded at the time as

223. Gołuchów. Castle

224. Gołuchów. Castle interiors

225. Grębień. Detail of paintings in the church nave

226. Gostyń. Dome of the Philipine church

a model of good urban planning. In the later part of the 19th century, however, the town's expansion became spontaneous and chaotic with tenement houses, factories, workers dwellings and sumptuous palaces of factory owners [234] appearing side by side and covering ever wider areas. After 1945 work began on restructuring the town; new residential districts were built and the central district underwent partial replanning to accommodate new public buildings and housing districs. (I.J.K.)

Łódź is the home of two museums with highly specialised collections. The Museum of Art, while also exhibiting older Polish and foreign works of art, concentrates on 20th century avant-garde artists.

The second museum, connected especially with the town's past and its specific character as a textile manufacturing town is the Central Museum of the Textile Industry, organised in 1960 in former factory buildings dating from the 19th century. Apart from exhibits relating to the industry's history, the museum collects Polish artistic tapestries. Rugs and tapestries from the 18th century are particularly noteworthy, as well as the decorative sashes so typical of Polish noble dress in the 17th and 18th centuries. A rich collection of contemporary, experimental tapestries by leading Polish artists is also housed there. (P.T.)

Jarocin evolved from a ducal market settlement. Municipal status was granted in 1257. Development was associated with trade and the crafts. After a period of depression in the late 17th and 18th centuries, life returned to the town in the later half of the 19th century. Today it is an important road and railway junction, as well as an industrial centre. The town hall [227] dating from 1799–1804 and a number of other interesting old buildings have come down to our times.

Situated at the meeting place of Wielkopolska, Małopolska and Mazovia, Piotrków Trybunalski also arose as a ducal market centre, and was granted municipal status in the 13th century. From the 14th to the 18th centuries it was an important political centre where the Polish nobility held its gatherings. From 1578 to 1792, it was the seat of the Crown Tribunal. The town was seriously damaged by fire and foreign occupation in the 17th and 18th centuries. Its economic and cultural importance grew again in the 19th century. Today Piotrków is a centre for the machine industries, glass and textiles. Historic monuments include Gothic and Baroque monasteries, a castle dating from 1511, 18th and 19th century merchants' houses and others. The province administration offices are housed in an impresive Neo-Classical edifice [236]. (I.J.K.)

227. Jarocin. Town hall

228. Kalisz

229. Poddębice. Manor house

230. Ożarów near Wieluń. Wooden manor

231. Łódź

232. Łódź. Freedom Square

233. Łódź. Piotrkowska St, art-nouveau houses

234. Łódź. Poznański palace interiors

235. Łódź. Geyer's factory

Łęczyca is located on the borderline between Wielkopolska and Mazovia. It is a small town today reputed for its ancient history and former glories. The older stronghold, on the site of Tum village, dates from the 6th to 8th century. Łęczyca was a centre for the Łężynianie tribe, which was included in the state of Mieszko I, and later it became one of the oldest castellanships in Poland. A Benedictine abbey was established here in the 11th century, and later belonged to the bishops of Gniezno. In 1161 a Romanesque collegiate church was consecrated on the abbey's site. In the 13th century Łęczyca became the capital of a regional principality, serving from the 14th century as province capital. Casimir the Great had the new town surrounded by defence walls and a castle was raised. The stone Romanesque defensive collegiate church is the most important single historic monument [237]. Rebuilt on several occasions, the church was bombed and burned in 1939. Postwar reconstruction has restored its historic appearance. (I.J.K.)

236. Piotrków Trybunalski.
     Voivodship Office

237. Tum near Łęczyca.
     Archcollegiate church

Mazovia and Podlasie Lowland

Warsaw, the capital and heart of Poland, is at the centre of the Mazovian Lowland. Traces of settlement reach back to the Bronze Age. In the 10th to 11th centuries the stronghold of Old Bródno developed on the Vistula's right bank while from the 11th century the settlement of Kamion with its left-bank twin, Solec, are known to have existed. The stronghold of Jazdów appeared in the 13th century on the Vistula's left bank, and by the end of that century, on the site of the present Royal Castle, a castellan settlement had sprung up. Old Warsaw evolved in the vicinity of the Castle Square at the turn of the 13th century [239, 240]. Market and craftsmen suburbs evolved simultaneously with the main township, including the New Town, or Nowe Miasto, which was excluded from the Old Town sheriff's jurisdiction in 1408. The town's importance was greatly enhanced by moving the ducal seat from Czersk to Warsaw in 1413. The town benefited from transit trade between East and West, and after 1466 mainly from the Vistula trade. Banking and the crafts began to develop in connection with trading. Following Mazovia's incorporation into the Polish Kingdom in 1526 and the Union of Lublin in 1569 Warsaw's political importance as a town in the very centre of the Commonwealth grew considerably. Chosen to be the seat of parliament and the site of royal elections, Warsaw became the country's royal capital in 1596. Sigismund III Vasa had the ducal castle rebuilt and extended into a royal residence. Growth ensued transforming the urban structure. The Market Square's Gothic town houses were rebuilt and enlarged in the Renaissance and Baroque styles [241]; the gentry and magnates built residences in the royal capital and even founded their own private townships which possessed separate municipal rights, they built their own churches and attracted their own residents. Praga evolved as a separate town on the river's east bank. The Swedish invasions of the mid 17th and early 18th century caused very serious damage and contributed to the merchants' impoverishment. Renewal came in the mid 18th century and especially under the rule of King Stanisław August Poniatowski, a great patron of the arts, literature and education. Trade expanded, as did the manufacturing industries and the banking system. Merchants built new houses while the gentry and magnates invested in palaces. Warsaw became a progressive centre of the Enlightenment. Political and social reform movements had their heyday in the May 3rd Constitution of 1791. The city itself was transformed and the private townships integrated into a single urban organism. The final Third Partition of Poland degraded Warsaw to the status of a Prussian provincial seat (1796–1806). Life returned to the

239. Warsaw. Old Town, panoramic view from the Vistula river

◁ 238. Mazovian landscape

city when it became the administrative centre of the Grand Duchy of Warsaw (1806–1815), set up by Napoleon, but a real regeneration came during the ensuing period of home rule when it acted as the capital of the Congress Kingdom (1815–1831). Economic life flourished, together with political and cultural activities. The city underwent significant rebuilding and a series of monumental structures in the classical style was erected. The University was opened in 1816, the Conservatory in 1821 and the Polytechnical Institute in 1826. The Society of the Friends of Science directed academic life, while the Polish Theatre was established in 1800. Conspiration against official and tsarist overlordship grew throughout the 1820s to culminate in the November Uprising of 1830–1831. Its disastrous failure led to the loss of political autonomy and to the closing of many institutions of higher learning. Cultural and academic life concentrated then in the remaining academic centres, the editorial offices of various periodicals and private salons. The theatres also continued to function. In 1844 the school of Fine Arts, previously housed in a university departament, was reopened, while the University itself returned to life in 1862 under the guise of the so-called "Main School". Artistic, literary and scientific patronage increasingly became the domain of the bourgeosie – in place of the aristocracy – reflecting greater economic activity and influence in connection with the industrial revolution. Warsaw became the seat of the National Government during the January Uprising (1863–1864). The collapse of this second major insurrection led directly to Warsaw's loss of intellectual and cultural primacy in favour of Cracow and Lvov although its economic ascendancy reached a climax later. The working classes became a very significant social group. Apart from issues of social and political emancipation, the citizens of Warsaw strove for the legalisation of private Polish schools and academic and artistic organisations during the revolution of 1905–1907.

Warsaw became the capital of an independent Polish state in 1918, and dominated most aspects of political, cultural and academic life during the interwar years. At this time, large-scale urban planning and expansion of municipal facilities took place. As Poland's main cetre of the resistance and the home of the largest Jewish community in Europe, Warsaw suffered dramatically during the Second World War. Its historic and cultural heritage in the form of monuments, works of art, book collections, archives and museums with few exceptions failed to escape annihilation. The city center on the left bank, where the Warsaw Uprising took place in 1944 was destroyed in more than 80% and around 800 000 civilians were estimated to have lost their lives. In spite of everything, the city remained the country's capital. It has been rebuilt as a modern city occupying a considerably enlarged area.

240. Warsaw. Old Town, panoramic view from the west

241. Warsaw. Market Square in the Old Town

242. Warsaw. New Town

Warsaw's historic architecture suffered particulary severe destruction, largely resulting from premeditated Nazi vandalism. The reconstruction program restored most of the highly valued monuments and strove to preserve entire elements of the historic urban plan. Thus, the Old Town with parts of its medieval walls was rebuilt, together with the New Town. Part of the Theatre Square with its collosal Grand Theatre was also restored as were the Bank and Castle squares, underneath the latter of which a Gothic bridge leading to the Old Town was unearthed. With the active cooperation of Polish communities living abroad, the Royal Castle has been rebuilt; it was truly a massive effort which also embraced the interior decoration [243] in which elements of the original castle, salvaged from the site during the occupation and after the castle's demolition by the Nazis, were reincorporated. (I.J.K.)

In the second half of the 17th century the principal architect operating in Warsaw and Poland was the Dutchman, Tylman van Gameren from Utrecht, who was brought to Poland by Stanisław Herakliusz Lubomirski in or around 1666. Six years later the architect was ennobled as Tylman Gamerski. Although he had been educated as a painter, Gameren proved a superb architect. Educated in Venice, his works nevertheless took on a true northern and even Dutch character. One of his main masterpieces realized in Warsaw is the Krasiński Palace [245], erected in the years 1677–1682 and completed by 1697. It is a supreme example of European Baroque architecture. The interiors, featuring an imposing parade staircase, an excellently proportioned general plan, perfect sculptural decoration, were carried out by Andreas Schlüter of Gdańsk, an artist widely reputed throughout Europe.

Another important example of Tylman van Gameren's architectural achievements can be found in the former village of Czerniaków in Warsaw. The church of St. Boniface (1687–1692) combines very modest exterior proportions with exceptionally rich interiors [260], where the architect succeeded in achieving an effect of monumentality. Frescoes, stucco work and gilding do not weaken the purity of architectural form, but, combined with exceptional light effects and music, achieve the aesthetic harmony of the mature Baroque. (P.T.)

The early 19th century architect, Antonio Corazzi, was of similar importance to Warsaw in his time as Tylman van Gameren was in the late 17th century. The Italian architect, brought to Poland from Leghorn by Stanisław Staszic, worked in Warsaw for more than

243. Warsaw. Royal Castle and Castle Square

244. Warsaw. Ballroom in the Royal Castle

25 years. Although lacking the exceptional talents of the Dutchman, and adopting a conservative, academic Classicistic style of designing, Corazzi demonstrated considerable skills as a town planner. He successfully closed off Krakowskie Przedmieście with his design of the Warsaw Friends of Science Institute [250], also known as the Staszic Palace. He was responsible for the Bank Square, lined on one side by a series of official edifices, and for lending a former market place its monumental proportions by designing the Grand Theatre [246], raised in 1825–1833. At the time of its completion this was one of the most advanced, but also one of the most gigantic theatre buildings in the world. (P.T.)

The church of the Visitant Nuns on Krakowskie Przedmieście has the most beautiful of all Warsaw church façades [248]. Although raised in two stages, in 1727–1734 and 1754–1763, and therefore reflecting two styles – the late--Baroque and Rococo – it is an exceptionally uniform design. Columns and cornices dominate the façade, below which the walls gently follow the concave and convex rhythm. The façade is monumental, yet extremely delicate, especially in its chiaroscuto effects. The Rococo interiors are equally harmonious. The architect's name remains uncertain; it has been suggested that Karol Bay or Jakub Fontana are likely to have been the designer. A monument to Cardinal Stefan Wyszyński placed in front of the church in 1986 was designed by the sculptor Andrzej Renes. (P.T.)

Important historic events are associated with the Koniecpolski Palace, which later belonged to the Radziwiłłs [247]. It was originally raised in the early 17th century and was redesigned in the 18th. The present façade dates from 1819 and was designed by Piotr Aigner. The monument to Prince Józef Poniatowski was placed in front of the palace in 1965. This monument to the leader of the Polish forces during the Napoleonic wars, perhaps more than any other in Warsaw, had a dramatic history before it was blown up by the Germans in 1944. An original work of the Danish sculptor, Bertold Thorvaldsen, it was replaced by a copy presented to the city by the inhabitants of Copenhagen.

◁ 245. Warsaw. Krasiński palace, view from the garden

◁ 246. Warsaw. Grand Theatre

247. Warsaw. Radziwiłł palace and Józef Poniatowski's monument

248. Warsaw. Visitant Nuns' Church and monument to Cardinal Wyszyński

249. Warsaw. Tomb of the Unknown Soldier

250. Warsaw. Staszic palace

A mark of the destruction wreaked upon Warsaw by the Nazi occupant is the Tomb of the Unknown Soldier [249]; what remains is part of the monumental late Neo-Classical Saxon Palace blown up by the Germans. (P.T.)

Another statue designed by Thorvaldsen and dedicated to Copernicus, was placed in 1830 in front of the Staszic Palace [250]. The palace, originally designed by Corazzi, was rebuilt in the 1890s as a Russian secondary school and Orthodox chapel in the so-called Neo-Byzantine style, and was redesigned in 1924–1926 in a modernist-Classical mode, although the original Corazzi design seen today was not recreated until after the palace's partial destruction during the Second World War and especially during the Warsaw Uprising in 1944. (P.T.).

The Ostrogski Palace [251], also known as the Gniński or even the Ordynacki Palace, on Tamka street has its origins in a castle raised at the turn of the 16th century. The new building was begun in 1609 by Janusz Ostrogski, although it was completed by Tylman van Gameran for the Gniński family. World War II inflicted serious dainges. The palace changed owners and users several times and today it houses the Fryderyk Chopin Society. The church of St.Alexander is located in the middle of the Trzech Krzyży Square. It is a Classicist copy of the Pantheon in Rome (1818–25, P.Aigner), reconstructed in 1886–1894, destroyed in 1944 and reconstructed anew in its primary form after the war [252]. (P.T.)

The restored Royal Road stretches from the Royal Castle to the Belvedere Palace [257], which is at the edge of Łazienki Park. This wooded area at one time was a hunting ground for the Mazovian dukes. In the early 17th century, a bath house was put up in the middle of a pond, rebuilt by Tylman van Gameren for Stanisław Herakliusz Lubomirski. The baths („łazienki") lent their name to the future park and a palace complex which was constructed here. The Baroque pavilion housing the baths was situated on an island surrounded by artificial waterways. In 1764 Łazienki were acquired by king Stanisław August. Avenues were laid out among the trees and the canals partially transformed into an artificial lake; new pavilions were erected. From 1775 the baths were extended in phases into a summer residence known

251. Warsaw. Ostrogski palace

252. Warsaw. Trzech Krzyży Square, St. Alexander church

253. Warsaw. Łazienki Park, Palace on the Water

254. Warsaw. Łazienki Park, Palace on the Water interiors

from then on as the Palace on the Island or the Palace on the Water [253]. New interiors were designed and richly decorated [254]. Two connecting pavilions on either side of the lake with bridges and colonnades were also constructed. These plans, prepared by the king, were realised by a large group of artists, including the architects Dominik Merlini and Jan Christian Kamsetzer, interior designers Jan Bogumił Plersch, Marceli Bacciarelli, Andrzej Le Brun and Franciszek Pinck. The Myślewicki Palace and Little White House [255] were raised in 1774–1776. The Trou Madame pavilion standing near the main palace was shortly rebuilt as the Little Theatre. An amphitheatre extending into the water was raised by the southern end of the artificial lake, while a guardhouse and enlarged outbuilding were built on the opposite side of the northern end.

The Orangery, housing a second, smaller theatre in its eastern wing, was constructed at the foot of the escarpment. The park was redesigned as an English Romantic garden by Jan Chrystian Schuch and ornamented with summer houses, small bridges and sculptures. The palace's southern prospect ended on a waterfall, while that to the north looked on to a statue of King Sobieski. The King visited Łazienki with his court during the summer months. Colourful theater performances were staged and the famous Thursday dinners at the Palace attracted the cultural and intellectual elite. In 1817 Łazienki passed into the hands of tsar Alexander I. New service buildings were put up in the 1820s, the Trou Madame pavilion was redesigned as the New Guardroom and the Great Outbuilding became the seat of the Cadets School.

The Łazienki Park and Palace complex remained virtually unchanged until 1939. Before the Nazis seized Warsaw some of the palace furniture and art objects were transferred to the National Museum. Following the collapse of the Warsaw Uprising, the palace was burned and the Nazis prepared to dynamite it; it was only a lucky coincidence that the buildings escaped complete destruction. Reconstruction began immediately after liberation. The Palace on the Water, Orangery and Little White House are all museum buildings now. The freestanding sculptures and monument to Fryderyk Chopin, designed by Wacław Szymanowski unveiled in 1926 [256], all destroyed by the Nazis, were restored. The Chopin concerts are held at the foot of the monument on Sundays in the summer months.

The Belvedere Palace and its complex above the escarpment are connected with the Łazienki Park. The original villa, almost certainly wooden, was raised in 1659 for Krzysztof Pac and was given the name Belvedere for the beautiful site and the view from it. The next owners, the Lubomirski, had a new, Baroque palace built there

257. Warsaw. Belvedere

255. Warsaw. Łazienki Park, White House interiors

256. Warsaw. Łazienki Park, monument to Frederic Chopin

(1730–1750) which after 1767 came to belong to the king, and following his death to his brother Józef Poniatowski. Bought in 1818 from the last owner, the Kicki family, by the Congress Kingdom authorities, the Belvedere became the residence of the tsar's brother, the Grand Prince Constantine. Between 1818 and 1822 the palace was extended to receive upper floors, a portico with four columns in the main entrance and garden facades and single storey wings along the sides of the front courtyard [257]. A landscape garden was laid out at the foot of the escarpment. Since 1918, the Belvedere has been the offical residence of the Polish President. (I.J.K.)

When in 1674 Jan Sobieski ascended to the Polish throne, he initiated the building of a suburban residence at Wilanów (which used to be called Milanów at that time). At first it was a single-storeyed manor house with alcoves, typical of the time, but this modest building was soon extended (1681–1682), probably under the direction of Tylman van Gameren. The final phase in the construction of Wilanów during the king's lifetime ensued in 1684–1696 under the guidance of a polonised Italian, Augustyn Locci. An extensive complex arose [258], composed of a main building, galleries topped with towers and palace wings on either side of the courtyard. Reputed artists, including the Gdańsk sculptors Andreas Schluter and Stefan Szwaner, the stucco decorator Joseph Belotti and brilliant fresco painter Michelangelo Palloni, Frenchman Claude Callot, as well as the two Poles, Jerzy Szymonowicz-Siemiginowski and Jan Reisner, educated in Italy at the king's expense, worked with Locci. The façades are characterictic of fully evolved Baroque, organically linking architectural, sculptural and painted elements. A parade courtyard was laid out on the palace's axis. Successive owners of Wilanów added to the original buildings and altered the gardens.

Wilanów today is composed of around seventy palatial apartments [259] reflecting interior decorations introduced in the 17th, 18th and 19th centuries. The only truly authentic Baroque residential interiors in Poland have been preserved here. The palace's partial devastation under Nazi occupation necessitated a costly and complex restoration program, during which numerous discoveries concerning the palace's past were made.

The impressive exterior and interior decoration relates to Roman antiquity, in line with Sarmatian ideology praising the virtues and great deeds of the king as well as the charms of his wife. Unlike most Baroque residences, the representative chambers are located on the groundfloor rather than the first storey, reflecting the failure to achieve true monumentality so typical of royal

258. Warsaw. Wilanów palace

259. Warsaw. Wilanów palace, King's antechamber

260. Warsaw. St. Boniface church interiors

residences of the times. Apart from the historic interiors, it houses a gallery of Polish portrait paintings from the 16th to 19th centuries as well as an exhibition of the arts and crafts in the former orangery. The building of the former riding school was adapted in 1968 into the world's first Poster Museum, now the location of the internationally acclaimed Poster Biennale competition. (P.T.)

The centre of Warsaw evolved far to the southwest of the medieval core during the 19th century, following the line traced by Marszałkowska Street as well as the intersecting Aleje Jerozolimskie. The streets were broadened during the postwar reconstruction and redevelopment, and Marszałkowska took on quite a different appearance from its traditional crowded character of prewar days. New public buildings [261], shops and housing districrs have been erected. The eastern side of the northern section of Marszałkowska is dominated by the immense Palace of Culture and Science, which is a monumental, pseudo-classicist skyscraper housing the Polish Academy of Sciences, numerous other academic societies, theatres, cinemas, exhibition halls, sports halls and a number of restaurants. The Congress Hall seats 3200 people. The „Centrum" department stores were raised on the opposite side of Marszałkowska between 1960 and 1969. Behind them there is a shopping district known as „Pasaż Śródmiejski". The Central Railway Station was built in the mid-1970s some distance from the intersection of Marszałkowska and Jerozolimskie Streets. The exterior building is comparatively modest, considering the extensive scale of underground network. (I.J.K.)

Among the more than 40 museums open in Warsaw, the most important is the National Museum, founded in 1862 as the Museum of Fine Arts. Its collections cover all periods from antiquity to modern times and embrace many cultures. The ancient art gallery presents works acquired from research sites explored by Polish specialists in Egypt, Syria, Sudan and Cyprus. Particularly noteworthy are the 71 Coptic paintings from the cathedral at Faras in Sudan. The gallery of medieval art exhibits works of art from various parts of Poland dating from the early 13th to the mid 16th centuries; it is the largest Polish collection outside of Cracow. The modern and contemporary art collections are a rich addition. The Warsaw realist school in painting from the late 19th century is especially interesting. The North European schools of painting are well represented, including those of the Netherlands, Germany and 17th century Holland.

261. Warsaw. Fragment of Bankowy Square with new office tower

262. Płock. Panorama

263. Płock. Art Nouveau Museum interiors

264. Opinogóra. Castle

265. Ciechanów. Castle

Many valuable works of art are to be found in the reconstructed chambers of the Royal Castle. Polish art is represented by portraits of monarchs and historic personages especially from the times of Stanislaus Augustus Poniatowski. The rooms are full of paintings, sculptures and objects of the decorative arts creating a display of period interiors. Płock, impressively situated on the high bank of the Vistula [262], is the oldest settlement in Mazovia. In the 8th-9th centuries it was the centre of a heathen cult and by the 10th century had become a ducal seat. In the 11th century, it was the seat of a castellanship, thereafter the centre of a bishopric. It was a residence of the ruling princes. In the 12th century Płock became the capital of a Mazovian principality, while the Duchy of Płock was established later on. Municipal status was granted in 1237. A new castle was constructed after the duchy's incorporation into the reunited Polish Kingdom under the reign of Casimir the Great, and the town was encircled with defence walls. The town flourished from the Vistula trade prior to its destruction at the hands of the Swedes in the mid-17th century. Płock did not recover until the late 18th century and then it was incorporated as a result of the Second Partition into Prussia. At this time part of the castle together with part of the defence walls was pulled down in connection with the laying out of the New Town. Trade revived in the later half of the 19th century, a small-scale industrialisation was instigated, and cultural and intellectual life was nurtured. Incorporated into the German Reich in 1939, Płock became an important centre of the resistance movement.

Płock's dynamic development since 1945 has largely been due to a huge petrochemical plant built in 1960. In under 20 years, Płock has been transformed into a major industrial centre with engineering works, food processing factories and timber plants, as well as the petrochemical industry. It is also an important river port and has its own shipyard. It has remained an important cultural centre. The old quarter is full of examples of old architecture. In the Museum of Mazovia, apart from archeological and ethnographic exhibits, the Art Nouveau collection is particularly notewortly [263]. (I.J.K.)

The Gothic castle of the Mazovian dukes at Ciechanów [265] was constructed in c.1429, on a rectangular plan with two circular towers. A two-storey residential building was originally located in the courtyard. From 1526, the castle belonged to the wife of Sigismund the Old, Bona Sforza. From the mid-17th century it started to decline and the residential building was pulled down by the Prussians after the Second Partition. The castle is an example of a regular, lowland fortress accommo-

208

dating today the town's cultural institutions.

An original example of the Romantic style in architecture is the small Neo-Gothic castle at Opinogóra [264], built by general Wincenty Krasiński according to plans drawn up by the famous French architect and conservator Eugene E.Viollet-le-Duc. An attempt was made to recreate the climate of the Romantic era by refurbishing the castle interiors in accordance with the style of the times and displaying personal effects of the Polish Romantic poet Zygmunt Krasiński. The castle forms part of a larger complex consisting of a church where the poet's tomb is located, a cemetery and a beautiful landscape park. Pułtusk was know as a castellan town belonging to the bishops of Płock already in the 13th century. It received municipal rights twice: in 1257, and then in 1339 after it was burned down by the Lithuanian army. Its rapid development took place in the 15th and 17th centuries when Pułtusk was considered to be one of the main economic centres. Trade in agricultural products and wood developed thanks to the advantageous location of the town on the river which served as the main transportation route to Gdańsk. Special attention should be paid to the Gothic collegiate church of St. Mary the Virgin, which was constructed around 1443 with Renaissance interiors and a tomb chapel for the bishops. A classic bell tower from the end of the 18th century rises above the town. [266].

The Kampinos Forest [267] is a forest, dune and marsh complex occupying the central Mazovian depression and stretching as far as the northwestern limits of Warsaw. The forest's natural richness and landscape qualities led to the Kampinos National Park being established in 1959. Nine selected reserves are included in the park. Two belts of sand dunes within the forest rise above the swampy lowlands. Pinewoods predominate and mixed forest are rare, although there are some oak and hornbeam woods, alders as well as peatbogs, meadows and sand grasses. Unstable, shifting sand dunes occur everywhere places where there is no vegetation. Kampinos originally belonged to the Mazovian dukes and later to the Polish monarchs. It became popular hunting ground once Warsaw had been made the royal capital. Aurochs and bears are no longer to be found here. Only the elk was reintroduced after 1945. The fauna inhabiting the remnants of the primeval forests hardly differs from that common to the Mazovian countryside.

Countless crosses, graves and cemeteries testify to the historical battles Kampinos was the scene of. In 1939 divisions of the Polish army retreated through the forest to relieve the besieged capital. Partisans had their base here. (I.J.K.)

266. Pułtusk.

The village of Brochów lies on the edge of Kampinos Forest. A Renaissance church with three circular towers [268] has survived there, originally built as a fortified church (1554–1561), with defense walls and bastions added in the 17th century. The parents of Frederic Chopin were married here, and the composer himself was christened in the church. The house in which Chopin was born is in Żelazowa Wola and was formerly an annex of the palatial residence of the Skarbek family. Chopin spent the first years of his life there. A small museum of the artist was established in the house in 1931 [269] Concerts of Chopin's music are given on Sundays by outstanding pianists. There is a park full of interesting specimens of trees and flowers and a monument to Chopin dating from 1894. (I.J.K.)

The fertile Łowicz land belonged to the bishops of Gniezno as far back as the 12th century, and from the 15th century to the primates of Poland who ruled it as a separate duchy. The principal town, Łowicz, was one of the oldest fortified settlements in the land of the Piast. Before passing into the hands of the archbishops, Łowicz was the property of the Mazovian princes and a castellan's seat. It was granted a town charter in 1298. At the turn of the 14th century the fortified settlement was turned into a fortress which in later centuries became the primate's residence of impressive proportions. When the Swedes came in 1655 they put up strong fortifications here. When they left it, they destroyed the castle buildings and the town. Taken by Prussia in 1795, Łowicz became the property of the government and in 1807 the Duchy Łowicz was presented to Davout, a Napoleonic general. In the 1820s, tsar Alexander I gave it to his brother Constantine; hence the title of Duchess of Łowicz assumed by Joanna Grudzińska, the latter's morganatic wife.

In 1829, Skierniewice and a few farms were added to the Duchy. The first tenant leases were issued to peasants in the duchy, who became comparatively wealthy. A rich folklore developed.

After 1838, the duchy belonged to the Tsars and the administrative centre moved to Skierniewice where the Russians had a sumptuous residence. Łowicz remained an important market and regional centre. Badly damaged in 1939, Łowicz was rebuilt and today is the centre of food and knitwear industries. The Łowicz Regional Museum has an interesting collection of folk art from the region.

The colourful costumes, which belong to a still living folk tradition and way of

267. Kampinos Forest

268. Brochów. Defensive church

269. Żelazowa Wola. Frederic Chopin's manor house

life, are displayed during the annual Corpus Christi procession [271]. Beyond the regional costumes, the specific qualities of the Łowicz region are reflected in its music, folk songs, carved figures in wayside shrines, beautiful cutouts, ceramics, charming decorations of the cottages and their furnishings complete with utensils [270]. (I.J.K.)

The great Polish Baroque architect, the Dutchman Tylman van Gameren, designed the palace at Nieborów for Primate Michał Radziejowski between 1690 and 1696 [272]. He also planned the French gardens. In the following century the palace interiors were redesigned and a series of outbuildings put up. Nieborów maiolicas were manufactured here between 1881 and the First World War. There are many examples of these decorative ceramics in the residence. In spite of later changes, Nieborów is a good illustration of a late-17th century palace with its 18th and 19th century interiors [273] featuring Polish and English furniture, eastern tapestries, Wedgewood and Sevres porcelain, innumerous portraits and a rich collection of old books in the library. The Venetian globes executed by Vincenzo Coronelli in the late 17th century are well worth the attention; they originally stood in Versailles. The ancient sculpture, tombstones and sarcophagi, urns and other objects in the palace and park are evidence of the Romantic period's love of the past. A landscape park was established in the mid-18th century. (P.T.)

But the most interesting Romantic park in Poland can be found a few kilometres away from Nieborów, at Arkadia. Designed in 1778 by the Warsaw architect Zug to suit the philosophical and artistic ideas of Helena Radziwiłł, it took shape over the ensuing forty-three years. In line with English models, it represents a combination of freely evolving nature and buildings of different epochs and styles, some of which were intentionally designed to achieve the impression of great age and ruination. The central architectural element is the Neo-Classical temple of Diana. The walls of the High Priests' House incorporate fragments of ancient buildings, while the Gothic House was designed, exceptionally, by the painter Alexander Orłowski. Other structures include an aqueduct, Greek Arch [274], Sybil's Grotto and others. The original notion of opening up interminable perspectives was dropped. Thus, by avoiding a dominant spatial accent, emphasis

270. Łowicz region. Cottage interiors

271. Łowicz region. Corpus Cristi procession

272. Nieborów. Palace seen from the gardens

273. Nieborów. Palace library

is placed on the expression of independence and charm. Retaining virtually all its original elements, Arkadia fully reflects the Romantic call for a return to nature. (P.T.)

Czersk, a fortified settlement from the 11th century and later castellan's seat, was the capital of the autonomous Duchy of Mazovia in 1262–1429. It was granted municipal status in 1350. Czersk became known for its cloth and beer, but also traded in corn and timber. The removal of the ducal residence to Warsaw, the changing course of the Vistula and later destruction caused by the Swedish invasions led to its rapid decline. Today it is a small settlement whose inhabitants are mainly engaged in fruit and vegetable growing. The ruins of the castle of the Mazovian dukes built in the 15th century in the Gothic style with two circular towers and a gatehouse, rise above the little town [275]. Archeological research has revealed the existence of a timber stronghold destroyed at the end of the 12th century and later transformed into a cemetery.

Pilica, a left-bank tributary of the Vistula, is one of the most beautiful rivers of the Polish Lowlands [276]. Its source is on the Cracow-Częstochowa Upland. Its lower course flows through a broad valley. From the northern verge of the valley one can admire an extensive view over the meadows and pasturelands bordering the river and the more distant forested areas to the south. (I.J.K.)

Sulejów, lying on both banks of the Pilica, is a centre for the rural area around it as well as a summer and tourist resort. The nearby woods and Sulejów artificial lake to the north of the town ensure healthy conditions. Already in the first half of the 12th century there was a customs house here. A fortified Cistercian abbey was established in 1176–1177 [277], founded by Prince Casimir the Just and closed in 1819. The church, a late-Romanesque stone basilica with a transept, was raised before 1232 and has been partly reconstructed. The eastern wing of a late-Romanesque chapel house and Gothic cloisters from the early 15th century have survived from the original monastery. Defensive walls with gates and towers have also remained together with an arsenal. A regional museum is open today in the chapel house, recording the history of Sulejów and its region. (I.J.K.)

The park and palace in Puławy, situated on the Vistula's high right bank, played an important role in Polish history and culture of the end of the 18th century. The Czartoryski family's aristocratic residence attracted many artists, poets and cultured people. Puławy competed at the time with the Warsaw of Stanislaus Augustus as a beacon of the Polish

274. Arkadia. Greek Arch

216

Enlightenment. The King had plans to set up a *Musaeum Polonicum* to gather works of art and historic souvenirs, but his plans were never put into life. The Czartoryski achieved such a goal in Puławy. In 1800, the architect Christian Peter Aigner built the Gothic House and Sybil's Temple in the park [278], the latter taking its model from ancient Rome. A collection of paintings, including a number by Raphael, Leonardo da Vinci and Rembrandt, was housed in the Gothic House. This collection was to be the basis of the Czartoryski Museum set up in Cracow. Sybil's Temple accommodated the mementos of Copernicus, Żółkiewski, Kościuszko as well as royal insignia and banners. It was Poland's first national museum and a source of patriotic hope during the long night of the partitions. (P.T.)

The church [279] at Radzyń Podlaski dated to 1641 is a typical example of Polish mannerism; its graceful body, supported by buttresses and possessing narrow windows relates to Gothic forms, a frequent attribute of mannerist art. The interiors feature stuccoed vaulting and the mannerist tomb of the Mniszech family. The palace at Radzyń [280] was initially erected for the Szczuka family by Augustyn Locci, famous for his work at Wilanów, in the end of the 17th century. The present shape, restored following wartime damage, reflects the extensions made by a renowned mid-18th century Warsaw architect, Jakub Fontana. The palace complex has a Rococo stamp, reflecting the best French models and representing the best example of this style in Poland. A beautiful, Rococo staircase, still partly in existence, was used as an example for other Polish residences. (P.T.)

Polesie is a flat plain extending to the west across the middle reaches of the River Bug between the Krzna and Wełnianka rivers. The water table is near the surface; in depressions peatbogs have been formed making some areas and remaining stretches of water inaccessible [281].
To the north of the Krzna's confluence with the Bug, the latter river leaves the Polesie to cut a deep valley through higher land. From the barrow on the Bug's high bank near the town of Drohiczyn there is an extensive view over the river valley and lands beyond its left bank [282]. This border region of Mazovia became the object of continuous battles with the Lithuanians in the 13th and 14th centuries. After the Union of Lublin (1569), the region was incorporated into the Polish Kingdom. The origins of Drohiczyn can be traced back to the times of an early Ruthenian settlement. In the 12th century the town was capital of the Duchy of Drohiczyn. From the early 13th century it belonged to Prince Conrad of Mazovia, who in 1237 brought the Knights Order of the Dobrzyński Brethren to this place. They were banished shortly afterwards by Daniel Romanovich, prince of Vladimir and Galich (Western Ukraine,

275. Czersk. Ruins of the castle of Mazovian princes

278. Puławy. Landscape park. Sybil's Temple

279. Radzyń Podlaski. Parish church

280. Radzyń Podlaski. Palace

formerly Eastern Galicia). Conquered by the Lithuanians in 1280, it remained in their hands for almost 300 years. Drohiczyn became Podlasie voivodship capital after the Union of Lublin. War damages and natural disasters in the 17th and 18th centuries resulted in the town's economic decline. It was also badly damaged during both world wars. Today it is a small handicrafts and trade settlement, proud of its vestiges of the past: a monastery complex of the Franciscans from the 17th century, a convent and church of the Benedictine nuns from the 18th century, a church and college of the Jesuits from the 17th century and an Orthodox Church built in the late-18th century, some old houses and a manor of historical interest. (I.J.K.)

Liw was a fortified settlement and castellans' seat. An initially wooden castle, it was built by the Mazovian princes and erected in brick in the late 14th century [284]. A trading settlement developed under its protection; referred to in later times as Stary (Old) Liw, it was granted municipal status in 1350. In 1446, Nowy Liw received its foundation charter. Both centres prospered from trade and both suffered during the wars in the 17th and 18th century. United into a single urban organism in 1789, the towns failed to recover and lost their urban status in 1869. Today Liw is a small market centre and a well-known resort deriving its popularity from the River Liwiec. Wide sandy beaches and shallow, pure waters have enhanced its recreational attraction, especially for children. (I.J.K.)

The Narew [285], Podlasie's chief river, and the Biebrza were at one time the only means of communication through the dense forests untrodden by man. Today the forest is incomparably smaller and growing in patches, having been cleared to make way for agriculture and meadows.
The Kurpie Forest [287], a mere vestige of the once vast Narew forests, has retained some of its primeval features, although there are new trees growing among the old. Some reservations have been created to preserve the forest's original character. Little has inevitably remained of the original wildlife. The Narew divides the Kurpie Forest into the Green (northern) and White (southern) Forests.
The Kurpie Forest belonged to the Mazovian princes, and then to the king. The forest inhabitants are probably the descendants of Mazovian settlers seeking refuge from the Sudavians, Lithuanians and Ruthenians. The Kurpie people, who were free subjects of the king, governed themselves by the bee keepers common law, which was not recorded in writing until 1559. They were ruled by a district head, elected from among the wild bee keepers. Apart from bee-keeping, the inhabitants based their livelihood on fishing, hunting, pitch-making, burning charcoal, distilling potash as well as digging for and processing amber. To this day,

281. Polesie Lubelskie

282. Bug river near Drohiczyn

283. Drohiczyn. Benedictine church

284. Liw. Castle

285. Narew river near Różane

the Kurpie women make linen cloth and woolen rugs. Isolated from the outside world, they have preserved a specific regional character in their architecture and costumes [286], which can be admired especially on religious holidays, for instance during the Corpus Christi processions. Cutouts, embroidery, characteristically patterned fabrics and ceramic goods are famous throughout Kurpie. (I.J.K.)

New methods of construction and the 20th century way of life have not spared traditional rural architecture. The folk open-air museum has been steadily introduced since the last war to preserve relics of wooden buildings from total annihilation. In 1963 the Museum of Farming was opened in a restored historic palace complex in Ciechanów. Its collections consist of exhibits presenting the history of agriculture in the northeastern lands of Poland. The open-air part of the museum was laid out in the former palace grounds and now it groups various examples of wooden rural architecture, including a village granary [290] typical of the regional style from the eastern Białystok province.

In the Middle Ages, the border zone between Mazovia, Lithuania and Ruthenia was covered with dense forests, vestiges of which are to be seen in the Augustów, Knyszyn and Białowieża forests. The Białowieża Forest has retained its primeval character. This is the best preserved forested area in Central-Eastern Europe, occupying an area of c.125,000 hectares. Numerous tree species include spruce, pine, alder, birch and oak. Undergrowth and many animal species abound in the forest as well. The western part of the Białowieża Forest lies within Poland's borders and occupies an area of 58,000 hectares. More than half this area is taken up by on oak and hornbeam forest [288] with linden and maple trees. Significant parts are taken up by mixed woodland (pine, oak and spruce). Pine trees predominate on sandy soils, but marshland forests of black alder prevail in undrained lowlands. Ash alder swamps stretch along the streams; also there are wet alder swamps, peatbogs and meadows. Fauna is richly represented in the forest; 11,000 species have been recorded.

The Białowieża National Park was created in 1921 on an area of 5069 hectares, 4747 hectares of which are under strict protection, situated between Narewka and Hwoźna near the Byelarus frontier. This area has a primeval character and boasts rich vegetation. There are numerous outcrops of ancient trees; fallen branches are overgrown with masses of lichen, toadstools and mushrooms. Numerous

286. Kurpie traditional costumes

287. Kurpie Forest ▷

animal species are found here: lynx, elks, beavers, wolves, wild boar, badgers, roe deer, stags, otters, ermines; among the birds, capercaillie, black grouse, goshawks, storks, black cranes, white eagles. The small rodents and insect-eating mammals are particularly interesting. The Park has become the natural habitat of the European bison [289]. Breeding reservations for bisons and tarpans are also located here.

Białowieża Forest originally belonged to the princes of Ruthenia, then of Lithuania, later to the monarchs of Poland. After 1815 it became the property of the tsars of Russia, and finally returned to the Polish state in 1921. It has seen many great hunting expeditions over the centuries. Before doing battle with the Teutonic Knights in 1410, King Władysław Jagiełło with the Lithuanian Grand Prince Witold organised a great hunt in the forest to supply their armies with meat. The hunt lasted almost six months. The barrels of salted and smoked game provided nourishment for an army of 100 000 men taking part in the Battle of Grunwald. An obelisk standing in the park at Białowieża village informs of the great hunt that took place on 27th March 1752 during which Augustus III watched 42 bisons and 13 elks and numerous other wild animals being hunted; it reflects the forest's importance for the royal court as a hunting ground.

Settlements began to penetrate into the forest starting in the 16th century, Large areas were cleared. The forests continued to provide the kingdom with high quality wood, animals and honey. Plunder policies and poaching during the Partitions resulted in more serious damages and German plunder policy in the First World War led to more than 5 milion cubic meters of valuable wood being removed. As a direct result of hostilities and poaching, the bison and elk became extinct; many other animals were slaughtered. In postwar Poland research was undertaken to preserve the fragments of natural forest still remaining and to reintroduce the European bison. The Second World War did not cause significant losses, although immediately following peace more destruction occurred in connection with the state's reconstruction. Consequently, the forest, while having shrunk in size over the centuries, has survived on a very large area. Many animal species, have disappeared; some, like the auroch, which had already become extinct by the late 14th century, forever. A campaign to restore the European bison to the forest proved a success. In 1938, barely 20 years after the havoc wreaked by the Germans, there were 30 bison in Poland, 13 of which were living in the Białowieża. Fifteen bison in all survived the Second World War. The herd since then has rapidly multiplied to

288. Białowieża Forest.

289. Białowieża Forest. Aurochs

such a degree that they have become too numerous to be supported by the Park. Some of the Białowieża aurochs have been moved to other reservations, others have been exported to zoological gardens in other countries; in some cases permission is even granted to shoot selected animals as game. The herd in Białowieża Forest now amounts to several hundred head, the majority living at large. Elk have also been reintroduced to the forest. (I.J.K.)

Tykocin, a border stronghold of Mazovia, was granted municipal status in 1425. It belonged to the Gasztołd family, later passed into the hands of king Sigismund Augustus, then Czarniecki. Dowry of his daughter Aleksandra, it passed into the possesion of the Branicki in 1665. It was under their patronage that a number of historical buldings was raised. The most valuable is the late Baroque monastery of the Missionary Fathers with the church of the Holy Trinity completed in 1749 [293]. The famous synagogue is older, dating from 1642, and rebuilt in the 18th centrury [294]. A veteran soldiers's home was opened in 1638, one of the oldest in Poland. Tykocin declined during the 19th century to the advantage of Białystok. Heavily destroyed during the Second World War, it lost its municipal status in 1950, but remains the most attractive Baroque-Neo-Classical complex in the region.(I.J.K.)

The main industrial and cultural centre of northeastern Poland, Białystok was most probably founded by the Grand Duke of Lithuania Gedymin in the 14th century. Together with Podlasie, it was incorporated into the Polish Kingdom in 1564 and passed into the Branickis' hands as part of the Tykocin district in 1663. Tylman van Gameren designed a Baroque residence for them in 1697. Between 1728 and 1758 the palace was enlarged and partly remodelled as an impressive aristocratic residence which has come to be known as the Versailles of the Podlasie region [292]. Commander-in-chief Jan Klemens Branicki stationed a military garrison in Białystok; he fouded a military academy, a school for estate administrators and a school for young men. He also built a hospital and a theatre, and encouraged the development of handicrafts and manufacturing. The town received municipal status in 1749. After Branicki's death it passed into the hands of the Potocki, then the kings of Prussia, and was annexed into the Russian Empire in 1807. Its 19th century expansion was connected above all with the textile industrial area developed by the Russians in the 19th century. In the interwar years, Białystok was a voivodship capital. The Second World War spelt extermination for the majority of Biały-

290. Białystok region. Granary near Białowieża Forest

291. Kruszyniany. Mosque

292. Białystok. Branicki palace

293. Tykocin.
Church of the Holy Trinity

294. Tykocin. Synagogue interiors

295. Knyszyń Forest. Supraśl valley

stok's citizens, as well as extensive destruction. Białystok owes its postwar speedy recovery to its expanded industrial infrastructure and the appearance of numerous administrative, scientific and cultural institutions. (I.J.K.)

Lithuanian princes often returned with prisoners from their military expeditions against the Tartars and settled these people in various parts of the Grand Duchy of Lithuania. Later generations forgot their language but retained the Moslem religion and separate customs. They proved loyal to their new motherland as proved by independent Tartar formations fighting in Poland's wars and insurrections. Two Tartar villages have survived within the frontiers of modern Poland, in the extreme eastern part of the Białystok province in an area once belonging to the Grand Duchy: Bohoniki from the 15th century, and Kruszyniany, given to the captain of the Tartar company, Kryczyński, by Jan Sobieski who owed his life to the Tartars following the battle of Parkany in October 1683 during the Viennese campaign. The wooden, twin–towered mosque in Kruszyniany [291] dates from the 18th century. The village also possesses a Tartar cemetery with tombstones inscribed in the Arabic as well as Latin alphabet. (I.J.K.)

In the northern part of Podlasie Lowland, between Białystok and Kolno, there are wide depressions comprising the Biebrza Valley, Poland's most extensive marsh and meadow land [296]. Bogs, an aftermath of changing climate conditions after the last Ice Age, were formed creating peat layers as thick as 7 m in places. The largest deposits are in the Biebrza river's floodplain. The peat provides material for insulation, manure, and fuel. The larger of the marshes which have remained in the Biebrza valley are known as Czerwone, Kuwasy, Ławki and Wizna marshes. Two strict peat bog reservations have been created in the Wizna marsh, while the Czerwone Marsh has been given over to an elk reservation [297]. Black grouse is among the rare species of fauna surviving in the marshlands, attracting hunters as well as tourists interested in observing the mating rituals of these birds [298]. (I.J.K.)

296. Biebrza. Marshland

298. Biebrza. Marshland. Black grouse

297. Biebrza. Marshland. Elk

Lakeland and Pomerania

North of the Biebrza Valley is an extensive outwash plain where 114 000 hectares of Augustów Forest extend, 6300 hectares of it in Lithuania [300]. Fresh pine forests predominate here, the pines being very straight and tall. There are large tracts of pine forest; mixed forests with spruce are less frequent. In the damper areas there are alder woods. The Nazi plundering policy and later felling explain the youth of large parts of the forest. Apart from timber, the Augustów Forest supplies considerable quantities of resin, blueberries and mushrooms.

The forest was a royal possession until the Partitions. As in Białowieża forest, stores of slaughtered animals were kept in the forest prior to the Battle of Grunwald. Sigismund Augustus and Stephen Bathory hunted here. During the January Uprising (1863–1864) numerous insurgent groups had their bases here as did the partisans fighting the German occupant during the last war. The Czarna Hańcza river [301] flows through the Augustów forest and this part of it is a well-known canoe route. The mouth of the Czarna Hańcza lies beyond Poland's borders. It is an extremely picturesque river with water so pure it is possible to breed salmon along almost all its length. The Augustów Canal [303] connects the Czarna Hańcza with the Biebrza-Narew river system to create a single water route through the northeastern Polish borderlands. The river provides one of the most attractive canoe routes in Poland, passing through lakes and the Augustów Canal to the town of Augustów, the main recreational centre in the Suwałki region. Surrounded by woodlands, the town is situated on the River Netta between lakes Necko, Białe and Sajno on the southwestern edge of the Augustów Forest. It developed around an inn founded in 1526 by Jan Radziwiłł on the main land route between Grodno and Prussia. In 1546 Queen Bona, wife of Sigismund the Old, suggested establishing a town to be named Zygmuntów after the royal heir, Sigismund Augustus. However, the new town came to be known as Augustów in memory of the future king's second name. (I.J.K.)

When, as a result of the partitions the Vistula estuary was cut off from the Polish heartland and Prussian customs duties essentially closed trade via the old Baltic ports, the idea was conceived to construct a waterway by-passing Prussia which would link the Vistula with the Niemen and the Baltic via the Narew, Biebrza and Netta by means of a network of canals. The Augustów Canal's initiator was treasury minister of the Polish Kingdom,

299. Great Masurian lakes

300. Augustów Forest. Spruce tree forest

301. Augustów Forest. Czarna Hańcza river

prince Ksawery Drucki-Lubecki. Ignacy Prądzyński was its designer. Work was started in 1825, but was interrupted by the November Uprising. Construction was later financed by the Bank of Poland and completed in 1839. The length of the canal between Biebrza and Niemen is 101 km, 19 km of which is now outside the Polish frontier. The regulated Netta River, the Augustów region lakes and regulated part of the Czarna Hańcza form part of the canal system. Eighteen stone locks were constructed raising the water level from the Biebrza to Augustów by 15 m and lowering it from Augustów to the Niemen by 41 m. The initial 20 years of the canal's existence witnessed great activity. Because no other links were ever completed and there was stiff competition from the railways, the canal lost its economic significance. The fact that the Biebrza and upper Narew are today unregulated means the Canal possesses no links with other water routes in Poland. It is used mainly for tourist purposes, although timber is still floated from the Augustów Forest to sawmills located on Lake Białe (White Lake) [302]. Boat trips are arranged for holidaymakers visiting the area. Since 1968 the Augustów Canal has been placed under protecttion as a monument of early-industrial water transport and engineering.

The forest is rich in fauna. Rare species include lynx, beaver [306, 304] and elk, as well as the blue hare. A beaver sanctuary has been established on Lake Wigry. Decimated already before the Great War, the elk herds returned to the forest after 1960 from the nearby Czerwone Marsh. Wild boar are numerous, just like deer and foxes although the wolf, which was still found in the area at the end of the last war, has all but disappeared. Bird life is in abundance, particularly the rare black stork [305], popular among the tourists. There are also many varietes of smaller mammals, amphibians, reptiles and insects, while fish continue to abound in the pure waters. Certain species are protected. (I.J.K.)

Lake Wigry, situated at the northern edge of the Augustów Forest, is generally regarded as Poland's most beautiful lake, 2187 hectares in area and reaching depths of up to 73 m. The lake's shape, ressembling the letter „S", extends about 18 km along its axis. The Wigry coastline is well-developed, there are numerous bays and peninsulas, of which the largest – Wysoki Wągiel – stretches about 4 km. The banks are largely forested, hilly and accessible. The clean waters are rich in fish. In the vicinity there are many smaller lakes which were originally bays of the Wigry. The largest of these – Białe Wigierskie – has an area of 100 hectares.

302. Augustów Forest. Białe lake

303. Augustów Forest. Augustów Canal

304. Augustów Forest. Tree cut down by beavers

305. Augustów Forest. Black stork

Wigry is composed of three parts known as „plosos", the westernmost of which, in the vicinity of Bryzgiel village, is the most varied with a high shoreline offering magnificent views from the south over inlets, splits and islands. The lower, northern shore of this „ploso" is bordered with thick forests hiding many small lakes, three of which are linked with Wigry: the Okrągłe, Długie and Muliste lakes. The central „ploso" of Wigry has low, forested shores with some deep inlets, while the third, northern section of the lake is dotted with villages. In the Hańczański Bay where the Czarna Hańcza flows into the lake, there is a beaver sanctuary known as Stary Folwark where rich water flora as well as fauna may be found. A second beaver sanctuary at Zakąty is at the northeastern end of the lake in the Krzyżaków Bay. Since 1989, Lake Wigry and its surroundings have been functioning as the Wigierski National Park. The lake's extreme beauty and still unspoiled natural surroundings attract amateurs of water sports and summer holiday makers who make good use of the leisure and recreation facilities offered here.

On the northern side of Lake Wigry there is the former Cameldolite church, now dedicated to the Immaculate Conception. It is visible high above the waters [307]. The Cameldolities were settled on an island, known as Queen's Island, by King Władysław IV Vasa. In 1704–45 the religious order raised a monastery complex and linked it with the mainland by creating a weir. The resulting peninsula became known as the Monastery Peninsula. The Cameldolites, banned in 1800, farmed, attracted settlers, set up sawmillls, watermills, breweries and an alcohol distillery, as well as forged iron from the local ruddy sods. The religious complex was destroyed twice during the world wars, but the Baroque church was restored. The ruined monastery buildings (the so-called Royal House and its hermitages) have been reconstructed recently to serve as a holiday hotel. (I.J.K.)

Originally, the territorial enclave bordered by the Great Masurian Lakes in the west and the Niemen-Biebrza valley to the east was inhabited by the Sudavians, a Baltic people closely related to the Lithuanians and Old Borussians. They made frequent sorties into the neighbouring Polish and Ruthenian provinces. During the 13th century, they were severely weakened by the retaliatory attacks of Poles and Ruthenians, culminating in annihilation at the hands of the Teutonic Knights. The Knights with their vastly superior weapons delivered the Sudavians the last blow in 1283, invading and seizing their lands. Vestiges of strongholds,

306. Augustów Forest. Beaver

307. Augustów Lowland. Wigry lake. Cameldolite church

burial mounds and local place names are all that remain of the Sudavians. Their lands were thickly forested and became the object of a continuous conflict between the Knights and the Lithuanians. The meadows, wild forest bees and richly stocked lakes attracted Lithuanian, Ruthenian and later Polish settlers. In the second half of the 17th century, the Dominicans and Cameldolites undertook the colonisation of the forests. In 1602 the Dominicans took the former estates of the Wiśniowiecki and Sapieha families from Jerzy Grodziński, together with a town called Juriewo. The town's name was changed to Sejny. Between 1610 and 1619, the Dominicans erected a church and monastery there, remodelled in 1760 in the late Baroque style [308]. The town of Sejny, a name derived from that of river, failed to recover from the Swedish devastation until the late 18th century.

At the close of the 17th century the Cameldolites founded a village at a crossing of the Czarna Hańcza river. Called Suwałki, it was granted urban status in 1715. In the Third Partition of Poland (1795) Suwałki passed to Prussia and the church estates were confiscated. In 1807, the region was incorporated into the Grand Duchy of Warsaw, while after 1815, as a part of the newly-created Augustów voivodship, it belonged to the Congress Kingdom. From 1837 onwards, the voivodship operated as a government unit with administrative seat at Suwałki; in 1866, the town became the seat of a governorate. It grew significantly during the 19th century [309]. The poetess Maria Konopnicka was born here in 1842. The town of Suwałki was incorporated into the Nazi Reich in 1939. Following the region's liberation in 1945, it was developed economically as a regional centre.

The most easterly part of northern Poland comprises the Suwałki Lake District; an area of moraine ridges strewn in places with boulders deposited by the glaciers which descended from Scandinavia. Cattle is grazed in the meadows and pastures on the hills. Owing to the difficulties in cultivating this type of country, agriculture is of secondary importance here [310]. Lying in deep depressions, the lakes of this region are mostly small, but extremely picturesque. The highest and most beautiful part of this lakeland area is embraced by the Suwałki Scenic Park including the deepest lake in Poland, Hańcza (108 m) [311]. The Smolnickie lakes, particularly Lake Jaczno [313] and nearby Kleszczewskie Lake [312] have a charm all their own. (I.J.K.)

308. Sejny. Church of the Virgin Visitation

309. Suwałki

310. Northern Suwałki region

311. Suwałki Lakeland. Hańcza lake

The central part of the Masurian Lake District, as well as its main tourist area is the Land of the Great Masurian Lakes, a wide meridionally extending depression. The lakes, linked by canals, form a levelled water system 116 m above sea level. They occupy an area of 486 sq.km, of which 302 sq.km belong to interconnected lakes. Lake Mamry, Poland's second largest expanse of inland water covering an area of nearly 105 sq.km, is composed of several parts bearing different names. The western part, known as Dobskie, is famous for the Island of Cormorants bird reservation where the birds nest. The series of Great Lakes ends in the south at Lake Nidzkie, forming a deformed letter „C" and surrounded completely by the Pisz Forest [315]. The lake shore accommodates a number of holiday centres, the largest of which is Ruciane at its northern end. Lake Nidzkie is connected by a chain of smaller lakes to Lake Bełdany, into which the River Krutynia flows [318]. This 90 km route passing through a number of lakes is popular among canoeists.

Lake Bełdany fills the southern part of a long post-glacial depression extending as far as the town of Ryn. The central part of this depression is occupied by Lake Mikołajki, while the northern parts are occupied by lakes Tałty and Rynski. Lake Mikołajki is linked to Śniardwy [316], Poland's largest lake, covering 11,383 hectares, but somewhat shallow averaging 5.9 m and containing four islands. To the northwest Lake Śniardwy is connected with the small Lake Łuknajno where a wild swan sanctuary exists.

At the narrow neck between lakes Mikołajki and Tałty there is the small town of Mikołajki [317], a former Masurian village greatly expanded in the late 19th century as a holiday resort in the heart of the Great Masurian Lakeland. The finger lakes of the Mikołajki group are linked with Lake Niegocin by a canal running through lakes Tałty and Jagodne. Lake Niegocin is wide but comparatively shallow and a favourite haunt for yachters. Many holiday centres have been developed here, as well as on the shores of lakes Mamry and Niegocin. The Masurian Lakes offer wonderful opportunities for inland sailing sports and water tourism. Lake fishing is widely practised there as well. (I.J.K.)

The Jesuit church and monastery at Święta Lipka [320] was erected in 1687–1692 among lakes and forests. Its designer, Jerzy Ertli of Wilno, conceived a three-aisled basilica with a fine twin-towered facade. The interiors have retained their late-Baroque character. The polychrome paintings by Maciej

312. Suwałki Lakeland.
     Kleszczewskie lake ▷

313. Suwałki Lakeland.
     Jaczno lake ▷

315. Pisz Forest near Bełdany lake

Jan Mejer of Lidzbark on either side of the organs dating from 1721 are worthy of particular attention. The artist revealed a great talent for building illusion; the architecture of the nave has been extended by a painted architectural scheme. The vaulting lends the effect of being transformed into a cupola supported on painted columns. The artist's grasp of geometry allowed him to create the impression that the observer cannot be entirely certain where the real architecture ends and ilusion begins. Mejer's work was inspired by superb Italian models of illusionistic paintings. The bishop's castle in Lidzbark Warmiński [321] for centuries served not only as a seat of the Polish bishops, but also as a significant Polish cultural centre extending to the furthest reaches of Warmia. Its last resident, the achieved poet and novelist of the 18th century Enlightenment, Ignacy Krasicki, was thrown out of the castle by the Prussians in 1795. The building stands at the confluence of the Łyna and Symsarna rivers and comes from the second half of the 14th century. It is a regular four-sided brick construction enclosing a courtyard [322]. A tower and three pinnacled towers decorating the corners date from the late 15th century. Ornamental cross-vaults as well as frescos coming from the 14th-16th century decorate the reception rooms on the first storey. The castle chapel reveals an unexpected Rococo decor conceived in the 1770s. (P.T.)

Warmia is a comparatively ancient province occupying the Łyna and Pasłęk tributary valleys. It received its name from an Old Borussian tribe, the Warms. In the 13th century, it was seized by the Teutonic Knights who established a bishopric there. In the 15th century, the gentry and the townspeople founded the Borussian Alliance in opposition to the Order's hegemony. An uprising against the Knights broke out in 1454. The Alliance gained control of a group of towns and called for union with Poland. The Polish monarch, Casimir Jagiellonian, decreed the unification of Borussia and the Polish Kingdom and declared war on the Teutonic Knights which ended after thirteen years of hostilities with the Teutonic state being divided. By virtue of the Peace of Toruń (1466) Warmia was incorporated directly into the Polish Kingdom and the rest of Borussia became a vassal state. Warmia belonged to Prussia and later to the reunited Germany from the first partition (1772) until 1945.

316. Great Masurian Lakes. Śniardwy lake

317. Mikołajki on Mikołajki lake

318. Krutynia river

319. Great Masurian Lakes. Dargin lake

Orneta, located to the west of Lidzbark, was first mentioned in chronicles in 1308 and was granted municipal status in 1313. In 1440 it was one of the towns belonging to the anti-Teutonic union. Under Polish rule it enjoyed prosperity and was expanded as a Renaissance and later a Baroque town. Orneta declined under Prussian rule imposed after 1772, although it recovered somewhat in the second half of the 19th century. The most beautiful historic building is the Gothic church of St.John the Baptist raised before 1379 and containing interior decoration from the 15th to 18th centuries [323]. The origins of Olsztyn [324], picturesquely situated amid hills and lakes, go back to 1334, at which time the Warmia Chapter built a castle in this poorly populated region. A settlement developed around the castle and was granted municipal status in 1353. Olsztyn also joined the Borussian Alliance. The period of Polish control was one of flourishing development, both economically and culturally. In the years 1516–1521, Nicholas Copernicus was the town's administrator on behalf of the Warmia Chapter. In 1520, he commanded the town's defence against the Teutonic Knights. Its incorporation into Prussia in 1772 negatively affected the town's economic life, although it again began to prosper when a railway junction and a large military garrison were located there. After 1911, it was a regency capital. Despite a germanisation policy, Olsztyn remained an important centre of Polish activity throughout the period and in 1921 became the seat of the Union of Poles living in Germany. Olsztyn suffered serious damage in the last phase of the Second World War. Since 1945 a voivodship capital, it has developed industry considerably, particularly during the 70s and 80s. The town was rebuilt and its cultural functions have also grown. (I.J.K.)

Pasym [325], 30 km southeast of Olsztyn in the Olsztyn lakeland, was founded by the Teutonic Knights. In 1386, it became a town which, although it had joined the Borussian alliance, was left in the hands of the Order after the Peace of Toruń, in that part of the Teutonic state known after 1526 as Ducal Borussia. The town's contacts with Poland were nevertheless strong and many Polish settlers moved here. Its pastors in the 17th century were Polish and trade with Poland was a very important part of its urban economy. In 1656 the town was destroyed by the Tartars and fell into decline. The construction of a sugar refinery at the close of the last century brought some life back to the town, which was devastated and seriously

320. Święta Lipka. Jesuit Church

321. Lidzbark Warmiński. Castle

322. Lidzbark Warmiński. Castle courtyard

depopulated at the end of the last war. In 1950, Pasym lost its urban status, but numerous relics of its happier past ranging from the 14th to 19th centuries have been preserved. An eastern-Baltic tribal stronghold existing from the 6th to the 11th century stands nearby. Olsztynek is also situated in the Olsztyn Lakeland. Founded by the Knights in 1359, next to a fortified castle, the town was originally within the territory of the long-extinct Old Borussian tribe of the Sasins. Settlers from Mazovia arrived here in large numbers during the 14th century, and the Polish element remained dominant until the Germanisation policies of Bismarck took effect. Pro-Polish sympathies were strong in Olsztynek during the Polish-Teutonic wars of the 15th and 16th centuries, although the inhabitants' efforts to achieve a union with the Polish Kingdom came to nothing. Olsztynek became an important centre of Polish Protestantism during the Reformation. In 1765 the widely-known lexicographer and defender of the Polish language, Krzysztof Celestyn Mrongovius, was born in Olsztynek. The town was seriously damaged during both world wars, although a number of old buildings have remained. The open-air museum is a much greater attraction with its many examples of regional architecture from Warmia and Mazury [326]. (I.J.K.)

A turning point in the „great war" between the Polish Kingdom and the Teutonic Order was the Battle of Grunwald fought in 1410 near the village of Grunwald (Tannenberg) to the south of Ostróda. It was one of medieval Europe's largest land battles. The two opposing forces threw massive armies into it: Polish and Lithuanian with Ruthenian detachments led by king Władysław Jagiełło, and Teutonic, swelled by knights of various nationalities returning from the crusades, led by their Grand Master, the Prince von Jungingen. Jagiełło's significant military victory, while producing no immediate results, ended the period of Teutonic expansion and cemented the political union between Poland and the Grand Duchy of Lithuania. The monarchy's prestige was greatly increased at European courts and the battle has remained alive in the memories of Poles. On the 550th anniversary of the victory a monument was raised on the battlesite [327]. (I.J.K.)

The Chełmno Lakeland, occupying a region bordering the Vistula, Osa and Drwęca river valleys, was fought over by the Old Borussian tribes and the Polish state during the Middle Ages. Conrad, prince of Mazovia, granted the Chełmno Land to the Teutonic Knights, who after subduing most of Prussia, used the region as a base for sorties into Poland. Their system of

323. Orneta. St. John the Baptist church interiors

324. Olsztyn

fortified castles ensured complete control over the province. Radzyń Chełmiński is a small town located in the Chełmiński Lakeland. Several monuments are worth seeing there: a Gothic church from the first half of the 14th century, a Gothic cemetery chapel from the 18th century and an Evangelical church from the 18th century as well. Ruins of the Teutonic Knights castle are the most interesting (328). Since 1224, the town was the property of Prussian bishops. In 1231 it passed under the authority of the Teutonic Knights who constructed a huge castle there. In 1410 it was won by the Poles. Radzyń joined the Borussian Alliance, but in 1466 it came back to Poland. The Teutonic castle was destroyed by that time in constant wars with Poland. In 1772 it was conquered by the Prussians, and was finally reurned to Poland in 1920. The Teutonic Knights had a residence in Gołub Dobrzyń [329] on the Drwęca river. Anna Wazówna's residence was set up here and the castle was remodelled in the Renaissance style. The frontier between the Russian and Prusso-German partitions followed the river, separating Golub from its former suburb of Dobrzyń, which at that time developed as a separate town. In 1950, Golub and Dobrzyń were merged to become the administrative centre of a new region, accelerating their growth. Golub, adapted to accommodate tourist and cultural needs, is used for various ceremonies. (I.J.K.)

Chełmno is the main town of the region. It existed as a stronghold as early as the 10th century, later becoming the seat of Piast castellans. In 1215, it became a missionary bishopric, established to introduce Christianity to the Old Borussians. In 1233, it received municipal status on the basis of a modification of the Magdeburg Law. In the 14th century, Chełmno joined the Hanseatic League and began to flourish as a trading centre, incorporated in 1466 into Poland as a voivodship seat. In 1386–1697, a branch of the Cracow Academy was opened there. Incorporated into Prussia in 1772, Chełmno remained an active centre for the Polish national movement in Eastern Pomerania. Chełmno is one of very few Polish towns where the urban layout and medieval defence walls have survived intact [330]. This valuable complex includes an extensive market place, and many historic monuments, the most outstanding of which include the Gothic parish church (1290–1333) and a 16th century Mannerist town hall raised on a Gothic lower level and decorated with ornamental attics [331], rebuilt in the 19th century. (I.J.K.)

325. Pasym

326. Olsztynek. Open-air folk Museum

Toruń [332] has preserved only parts of its defence walls, mainly on the Vistula side, but its complex of medieval buildings rivals few other European cities and towns in our times. The urban layout comes from the mid 13th century and more than 350 Gothic buildings remember the times. Although lying some 200 km from the Baltic coast, Toruń was able to flourish from international „early-capitalist" trade thanks to the Vistula being navigable up to this point. Toruń joined the Hanseatic League, and its inhabitants began to oppose Teutonic rule, under which they were forced to pay extremely high taxes and tolerate restrictions on the trade with Poland. As the most important urban centre to be directly incorporated into Poland in 1466, Toruń became a major centre of the Protestant Reformation in the 16th century.

The impressive volume of the post-Franciscan church of the Virgin Mary [333] coming from 1350–1370, dominates the Old Town skyline. Initially, each of its three aisles was covered with a separate roof; the present one dates from the 18th century. This is a hall church with a ceiling 27 m high presenting an original construction rarely occuring in Gothic architecture. The nave, usually supported by powerful buttresses, in this case has smooth exterior walls and buttresses inside. The inside walls have been covered with a polychromy from the 14th century depicting scenes from the New Testament, while the star–and–flower motifs of the vaulting symbolise heavenly paradise. The graphic style suggests the artists were connected with or influenced by Czech art. The early Baroque tomb of Anna Wazówna, sister of king Sigismund III Vasa, was designed in 1636.

A large part of the Old Town Square is taken up by the town hall [334] which originates from the late 14th century when several of the buildings, including the cloth halls, storage buildings, stalls, town scales and law chambers were combined into one. The Gdańsk architect Antoni van Opberghen extended the town hall in the early 17th century, adding gables and corner pinnacles. The town hall of Toruń with its fine proportions and exterior niched-walls is reminiscent of late-Gothic town architecture from the Low Countries. The interiors were redesigned in the 18th century but have retained much of their medieval character, serving as an excellent background to the rich collections of the Toruń museum: medieval art, objects of the decorative arts and some Polish art from the 19th and 20th centuries. (P.T.)

327. Grunwald. Monument to the victory over the Teutonic Knights

328. Radzyń Chełmiński. Castle

329. Golub Dobrzyń. Castle

330. Chełmno

331. Chełmno. Town hall

332. Toruń. General view from
the Vistula river

Of the three Gothic churches, St. Jacob's in the New Town is worthy of special attention for its beautiful, slim silhouette dating from the years 1309–1321, best viewed en face from the closed presbytery. The architectural decor was enriched by glazed ceramic details with polychromy. The interiors [337] contain valuable furnishings from the 14th to 18th centuries, including Gothic frescoes, paintings and sculptures.

One of the Gothic town houses to survive is the house in which Nicholas Copernicus was born in 1477 [335]: a typical example of town residential architecture from the Hanseatic period, including gable and niches, a colourfully ornamented. Another house [336] in the Old Town Square displays a Baroque façade from 1697 featuring rich floral motifs. The „House Under the Star" which presently houses the Museum of Oriental Art has preserved a beautiful spiral and wooden staircase. (P.T.)

A view of Grudziądz from the river [338] reveals the picturesque complex of warehouses, most of which originate from the Middle Ages and which at one time formed part of the town's defence walls. From the late 13th century until 1466, Grudziądz belonged to the Teutonic Order, after which it became a royal town and venue for political gatherings of the Royal Borussian gentry. (P.T.)

Kwidzyń, was built in the earlier half of the 14th century under the protection of its castle, which was curiously connected with the cathedral [341]. A bishop's seat was created there in 1284. The castle took the plan of a regular square with four corner towers and an inner courtyard with galleries. An elevated gallery leads to a lateral tower known as a dansker. The cathedral was fortified, containing a twin-aisled crypt beneath the presbytery. A mosaic dating from 1380 has survived above the porch, as well as Gothic polychromy inside. (P.T.)

The Teutonic Knights' main castle-residence at Malbork (Marienburg) was raised in several stages. The earliest buildings, on the side of the River Nogat [339], were constructed at the end of the 13th century. In 1309, the Grand Master moved his residence permanently from Venice to Malbork. The fortifications were intensively enlarged during the 14th century, while the Great Refectory was raised in the middle castle [340] together with the Grand Master's residential building and the church of St.Bartholomew. At the end of the 14th century a four-storey residential tower was constructed with summer and winter refectories containing high vaults on granite supports. The Virgin Mary chapel is an exceptionally

333. Toruń. Virgin Mary church

334. Toruń. Old Town hall

252

valuable example of Gothic art, added onto the great chapter house. The castle was encircled by four lines of fortifications. Poland took control of it in 1457; it thereafter served as a seat for the local administrator. The castle, ironically, suffered its greatest decline under Prussian rule when it was adapted into a storehouse and barracks. Architectural details were damaged. Only after 1917 a gradual reconstruction of Malbork took place. It was continued after 1945 when the castle suffered disastrous damage. Today the former Castle of the Teutonic Knights represents the largest fortified complex in Europe. It has been turned into a museum presenting marvellously executed architectural constructions and details. (P.T.)

Gniew [342] situated on the left bank of the Vistula, was an old Pomeranian stronghold. In 1229, the Gniew Land was granted to the Cistercian Order of Oliwa and in 1276, under the last will and testament of the Pomeranian prince Sambor, passed into the hands of the Teutonic Knights, becoming their first bridgehead on the Vistula's west bank. Gniew became the main centre of the Knights' resistance. After its return to Poland in 1466, the town prospered thanks to the corn and timber trade. It was a royal administration seat, which in the years 1667–1699 belonged to the Sobieski family. King Jan III Sobieski often stayed there and built a Baroque palace in the castle approaches. The town later lost its importance. Badly damaged in the last war, it has preserved its medieval layout, parts of its defensive walls, a 14th century Gothic parish, late Gothic houses on the Market Place (14th and 15th centuries) and the Gothic castle, remodelled in Sobieski's times. (I.J.K.)

The Elbląg Elevation [343] lies to the southeast of the Vistula estuary: a gently undulating series of low hills covered with beautiful forests of beech and oak. The central part has been given over to agriculture. The significant industrial town of Elbląg lies on the river of that name, between the hills and the Vistula floodplain. It lost its importance as a large port and Hanseatic League member in the 17th century when its port dried up, but witnessed a revival in the mid-19th century when industrialisation followed the opening of railway links, as well as the digging of the Elbląg Canal which dates from 1845–1860 and connects it with Ostróda via a series of lakes belonging to the Iława chain as well as the shallow Lake Drużno which once formed part of

335. Toruń. Gothic town houses with the house of Copernicus

336. Toruń. Baroque houses, „Pod Gwiazdą" house

337. Toruń. St. Jacob church interiors

the Baltic Gulf. A great curiosity is the system of locks allowing boats to be transported over different levels of the water route. The canal today is used almost exclusively by tourists. (I.J.K.)

Frombork at the eastern end of the Elbląg Elevation was a seat the Warmia Chapter from 1278. Nicholas Copernicus lived and worked there in 1512–16 and 1522–43. It was here that he wrote his most important work: „*De revolutionibus orbium coelestium*". The buildings of historical interest in Frombork are the magnificent Gothic cathedral [344] built in 1329–1388 and a tower dating back to the late 14th century containing rooms where Copernicus lived and worked. In 1973, on the 500th anniversary of the astronomer's birth, a monument to his memory was unveiled in front of the cathedral. (I.J.K.)

The Vistula Estuary is separated from the open sea by a sand bar extending some fifty kilometres, created over the centuries by wind and wave action. To the west, the so-called Vistula Split separates the Bay of Gdańsk from the Vistula delta area, referred to as the Żuławy Fens. In the 13th century the estuary penetrated considerably further southwards linking up with Lake Drużno. In the 12th and 13th centuries, the higher ground amid the marshes was already settled. In the 14th century the Teutonic Knights directed the first draining projects, implemented on the eastern side. They encouraged settlers from northern Germany, Friesland and the Netherlands – experienced in the draining and drying of land – to carry out the work for them. The river banks were regulated, embankments, canals and ditches were formed. Windmills to work the pumps were built. The fens were subdivided into polders which were cultivated. By the 16th century, the Żuławy Fens had become known for their high level of agriculture, supplying Gdańsk, Elbląg, Malbork and more distant towns with food.

In the 19th century, the old dippers and pumps driven by windmills were replaced by steam pumps, which in turn were replaced in our own century by electric pumps. Following centuries of man's activity, the entire delta area was drained, i.e., 174 000 hectares, of which 47 000 hectares had been low-lying land of up to 1.8 m below sea level. At the end of the Second World War, as a last expression of desperation, the Nazis blew up the embankments causing 40 000 ha of farmland to be flooded and a further 32 000 ha to become waterlogged. The resulting bogs became

338. Grudziądz. General view from the Vistula river

339. Malbork. Castle, view from the Nogat river

340. Malbork. Great Refectory in the castle

341. Kwidzyn. Castle and cathedral

overgrown with reeds reaching three metres in height; in effect the fens looked not a great deal differently than six centuries earlier. In spite of many difficulties, the Fens were drained again by 1949, the drainage installations being modernised at the same time. Many state farms were set up in the area. Today wheat, sugar beet and rape-seed are cultivated on the Żuławy Fens, while cattle is grazed in the pastures and meadows. A great deal of historic architecture has been preserved in the fenlands; there are windmills of the classic Dutch model [345] and half-timbered churches and houses, many of which feature arcades [346]. (I.J.K.)

Gdańsk [347] is Poland's largest port. Its origins go back to 997, when it was first recorded already as a part of the first Polish state ruled by Mieszko I. By the 12th century it was a well-organised port town handling considerable traffic. During the feudal period, Gdańsk was the capital of an independent duchy ruled by the Pomeranian princes. In 1225, it was granted municipal status according to the Law of Lubeck. After capturing Gdańsk in 1308, the Teutonic Knights enlarged and remodelled the former castle of the Pomeranian princes as a residence for the commander of the Order. During the 14th century four independent urban organisms grew up around the castle. The settlement of Osiek was granted urban rights by the Knights in 1312; lying nearest to the castle, it was settled by fishermen and craftsmen who moved from the Old Town destroyed in 1308 [349]. In 1343, the Main Town was founded on the River Motława [348] and was destined to become the central district in the future. The town expanded and gained power rapidly, joining the Hanseatic League. From 1374 there is again mention of the Old Town as a restored community, and in 1380 the Knights founded the New Town to the north of the castle.

The port was expanded and the Great Mill was built on the River Radunia in 1364. After the Grunwald victory, Gdańsk paid homage to the king of Poland and in 1440 joined the Borussian Alliance. Fourteen years later, the citizens took up arms against the Teutonic Order. In the ensuing years, the city, now incorporated into the Polish Kingdom, participated in the war against the Knights, supplying the king with money and armed forces.

Granted a royal privilege in 1457, the four separate towns were joined into a single urban organism. In the course of the following centuries, Gdańsk was granted many privileges and maintained considerable independence within the Polish-Lithuanian Commonwealth. The port expanded toge-

342. Gniew. General view

343. Elbląg Elevation. Landscape

344. Frombork. Cathedral and Nicolaus Copernicus monument

345. Żuławy. Arcaded house in
Marynowy village

346. Żuławy. Windmill

347. Gdańsk. Long Shore

348. Gdańsk. Main Town

ther with the town. A storage district developed – known as the Island of Granaries – on the other side of the Motława, while the Lower Town arose on the more distant banks of the Nowa Motława and the Old Suburb evolved south of the Main Town, partly in response to the New Town's destruction after 1455.

The Reformation found a vital base in Gdańsk, and in the period 1525–1577, the townspeople rebelled a number of times against Polish overlordship. The greatest economic and cultural development occurred in the early 17th century, coinciding with Poland's own „Golden Age". At this time 80 percent of the Commonwealth's foreign trade was concentrated in Gdańsk, which exported corn, timber and other agrarian products floated down the Vistula from the far corners of Poland. At the same time Gdańsk became an important production centre, making cloth, furniture, metal goods, paper and arms, which were stored in the Great Armoury [356] put up in 1603–1605.

The Swedish Wars undermined the urban economy seriously. Recovery was never full afterwards. In 1793, Gdańsk was incorporated by force into Prussia and most of its former privileges were lost. The port was considerably extended in the second half of the last century; railway lines were laid and the shipbuilding industry expanded. Between the wars Gdańsk-Danzig was a Free City. It suffered heavy destruction in the closing months of Ward War II; ironically, the historic quarters were the most severely affected. The city's historic monuments were restored with great attention after 1945. The most impressive ones form a magnificent complex in the Main Town, dominated by the late Gothic Church of the Virgin Mary [351] raised in stages between 1347 and 1502. (I.J.K.)

In 1612–14, Abraham van den Blocke designed the Golden Gate [350] closing the view of Długa Street. The bright stone elevation with the classical column and entablature arrangement suggests Italian influence, although this would be a superficial supposition. The stone lintels decorated with circular and cone-shaped motifs reflect the Mannerist spirit of this monument. The restored sculptures adorning the balustrade represent personifications of Peace, Freedom, Wealth and Fame.

The residence of the St. George Brethren is next to the Golden Gate. It was raised in 1487–1494 by Georg Glotau, replacing a demolished section of the defence walls. It is an exceptionally beautiful and very late Gothic building featuring an exquisitely composed

349. Gdańsk. View from Grodziska towards the Old Town

350. Gdańsk. Main Town, Golden Gate, and the house of the Brethren of St. George

351. Gdańsk. Main Town. Virgin
     Mary church

352. Gdańsk. Long Market and town
     hall in the Main Town

façade and official chamber on the upper floor.

The Gothic Arthur's House originates from a 15th century patrician's residence rebuilt in connection with an official visit of king Sigismund Augustus to the city. The house received its present look in 1616–18 when Abraham van den Blocke adapted the Gothic façade by introducing northern Mannerist forms. The portal is decorated with figures of Sigismund III and Władysław IV, statues of classical heroes renowned for their integrity and sacrifice for their homeland, personifications of Justice and Might, which are located in the lower part of the gable, and a figure representing Fortune crowning the gable. The sculptural program reflects the ideology of Gdańsk patricians who had their seat in the house: that the goodwill of ruling powers and the virtues of the city's inhabitants will secure eternal success for the town. A final element in this program is the fountain standing in front of Arthur's House with the figure of the God of the Seas, Neptune, also designed by van den Blocke the Younger in 1604 (unveiled in 1633). (P.T.)

The Main Town Hall [352] on the Long Market (Długi Targ) was Gdańsk's most important public building. Its oldest part dates to 1379–1382, although its present shape and lofty tower clearly refer to the late-medieval town halls of Flanders and the Netherlands, and come from the 15th century. When the Gothic spire burned down, Dirk Daniels designed a Renaissance tower erected in 1561 and crowned by a golden figure of Sigismund Augustus, together with a carillon of bells. Anton van Opberghen, architect of the Armoury, redesigned the main facade in a Mannerist spirit and totally refurbished the interiors. Burned and partly demolished in 1945, the town hall was not restored in full; only the main chamber, known also as the Red Room, regained its original decor [353]. This is the most successful interior Mannerist design in Poland, conceived almost entirely by Flemish-Dutch artists between 1591 and 1611. Willem van der Meer of Ghent created the wonderful hearth, Hans Vredeman de Vries painted a series of allegorical scenes to decorate the walls, while Isaac van den Block, son of the sculptor Willem, conceived the ceiling ornamentation with its unique collection of 25 paintings dominated by the *Apotheosis of the Union of Gdańsk with Poland*. The Red Room relates in style and program to the Doge's Palace interiors in Venice, the unparalleled model at that time for all port cities in

353. Gdańsk. Red Chamber in the Town hall

354. Gdańsk. Crane on Motława river

Europe. The paintings were delicately framed by Simon Hoerle, author also of the inlaid doors and benches. The Red Room interior decoration presents a complex and well conceived program reflecting the moral and political ideals of the townspeople of Gdańsk. (P.T.)

The beautiful late-Gothic brick gables belong to the post-Franciscan church of the Holy Trinity [355] raised in the late 16th century in the Old Suburb, although the chapel of St.Anne is somewhat older. The National Museum is located in the Gothic chambers of the former monastery.

The port of Gdańsk expanded historically in connection with growing international trade; by the mid-17th century Gdańsk was handling over two thousand ships annually. The port on the Motława had to be greatly expanded in the 14th century and in the 17th century a new port was constructed at the mouth of the River Leniwka. Most of the surviving architecture connected with the historic port had to be rebuilt after 1945. The Crane on the Motława [354] is a particularly valuable relic, created in the mid-15th century from a twin-towered Gothic gate accommodating a wooden port crane which had to be rebuilt after the war.

Shipbuilding represents the most important branch of Gdańsk industry. The Gdańsk Shipyard constructs a number of models of ocean liners, merchant and fishing vessels, for the home market as well as foreign clients. In 1980, the Monument to the Fallen Shipyard Workers was erected in front of the shipyard gate [357] to commemorate the tragic events of the 1970 strikes. It is a symbol of the changes taking place in Polish public life during the last decade or so. It was in Gdańsk in August 1980 that the independent trade union Solidarity was born to expand in time into a social movement which was to culminate in 1989 in the fundamental changes brought about in Poland, putting an end to the communists' monopoly on state government.

The port was extensively destroyed in the last war. In July 1945 the first ship entered it after the war. In the 1970s, construction of the Northern Port started; it receives the largest ocean-going vessels of modern times [359] carrying loads of mainly coal and liquid fuels.

At dawn on 1 September 1939, the first shots of the Second World War were fired in Gdańsk. They came from the German battle ship „Schleswig-Holstein", which had just arrived in the port on an official visit. Heroic resistance was put up by the employees of the Polish Post Office and a small force at the shipping depot on the sand bar called Westerplatte, which resisted the

355. Gdańsk. Old Suburb.
      Post-Franciscan church gables

356. Gdańsk. Armoury

357. Gdańsk. Monument to the Fallen Shipbuilders

358. Gdańsk. Monument to the Defenders of Westerplatte

359. Gdańsk. North Port

enemy for seven days before running out of arms and having to surrender. In 1966, a monument was put up as a tribute to the courageous defenders of the post [358]. (I.J.K.)

The history of museums in the city has been connected with the post-Franciscan monastery since 1848. The cross-vaulted interiors are among the most beautiful Gdańsk has to offer and provide a harmonious background to the rich medieval collectioons, including above all *The Crucifixion* from Starogard and *St. George* from Arthur's House in the Main Town.

The partly preserved 19th century collection of Jakob Kabrun is housed in the Museum today. It is composed of paintings, drawings and illustrations coming mainly from 17th century Flemish and Dutch schools. Earlier art from the Low countries is best represented by a masterpiece considered to have been the work of Hans Memling: a triptych entitled *The Last Judgement*. The arts and crafts collection is extraordinarily rich, particularly exhibits from Gdańsk workshops which from the 14th century were renowned in Poland for their gold, furniture, metal and ceramic products. Liturgical gowns from the 14th-16th centuries, and 17th and 18th century Gdańsk furniture is also excellently represented, as well as European faïences, including some rare Swedish examples.

A gallery of Polish art ranging from the 18th to 20th century is also housed in the Museum.

The illustrations present Gdańsk arts and crafts. The massive oak wardrobe dates from the beginning of the 18th century, a peak period in the city's furniture trade when plant motifs were applied.

In the 18th century, Gdańsk was a major centre of ceramics production. Beautiful tiled stoves were made here along with faience, the latter being distinguished by pseudo-Chinese scenes of daily life and fantastic fauna, painted on a white background.

In the 17th century gold crafts were particularly developed and Gdańsk artists were mainly responsible for the gold work of this time coming from the former lands of the Polish-Lithuanian Commonwealth. Numerous pots, frequently of great dimensions, were also executed in Gdańsk, richly decorated with coins and medallions. (P.T.)

360. Gdańsk. Cathedral in Oliwa

361. Sopot. Pier

362. Gdynia. Port

Gdańsk and the neighbouring towns of Sopot and Gdynia constitute a single urban agglomeration known as the Tri-City. Sopot fulfills a different role than the two larger cities: it is a popular seaside and spa. It developed from an old fishermen's village belonging to the Cistercians from the 13th century until the partitions. From the mid-16th century it was a favourite resort of the Gdańsk townspeople, although it achieved urban status only in 1901. It later developed as a fashionable resort. Affluent tourists willingly visit the Grand Hotel known for its excellent cuisine. The extended pier [361] reaching out 512 m into the sea is very popular among holiday makers, as is the only forest opera in Poland, beautifully situated among hills where an annual international song competition is held.

Gdynia, a former Cistercian village (from the 12th to the 18th centuries) is a large town and one of Poland's three main ports. The Polish authorities decided to build a new port [362] failing to secure favourable conditions in the port of Gdańsk in 1920. In 1923, a ceremony was held in which Gdynia was declared „a temporary military port and harbour for fishermen's vessels". In 1926, Gdynia received urban status and expanded until 1939 as one of Europe's most modern and largest ports. The port was almost completely destroyed by the retreating Germans in March 1945 and its entrance was blocked by the scuttled wreck of a German ship. The port was reopened as early as April 1945. The town and the shipyard were reconstructed. Today it functions largely as a small-scale loading and off-loading site; vessels of the largest tonnage are constructed in the shipyard.

The Hel Peninsula is an attractive area for summer tourism, jutting out some 34 km into the Bay of Gdańsk. A number of fishing settlements turned seaside resorts are located here. Hel lies at the far end of the penisula; it is an old fishing village founded as early as 1128. It contains a Gothic 14th -15th century church, adapted as the Museum of Fishing, an 18th century inn and timber-framed fishermen's houses from the 19th century [364]. A port was constructed here in the last century; after 1918 Hel developed as a spa.

Jastarnia dates back to the 16th century and maintains its traditions as a fishing settlement, although today it is primarily a spa. The most luxurious bathing places are Jurata and Kuźnice, former villages incorporated into the town in 1954. The Hel Peninsula has been created by wind and sea action, piling up sand-dunes which have become stable through natural and man-made afforestation of pine trees. Beaches stretch along both sides of the Peninsula; the ones facing the sea are narrow but sandy [363] while on the side facing the bay they are wide and pebbly. (I.J.K.)

363. Hel Peninsula. Beach in Kuźnice

364. Hel. Old fishing houses

365. Kartuzy. Former convent church

366. Pelplin. Cathedral

The Cistercian monks are responsible for two of the most valuable architectural monuments on the Gdańsk seaside: the monastery at Oliwa dating back to 1188 and that at Pelplin founded in 1274. Both are cathedrals today. Oliwa Cathedral [360] has a slim Baroque façade sandwiched between two Gothic towers crowned with spires. The late-Romanesque building with a transept, surviving in part in the narrow south aisle, was constructed in the early 13th century. Following a fire in 1350, the church was significantly extended and elevated, while the presbytery received an ambulatory and a rectangular monastery was added on the south side. The interior furnishings come from the late-16th to late-18th centuries and are a result of the Counter-Reformation offensive. A large collection of paintings and sculptures associated with the Mannerist and Rococo styles has survived; the former main altar is located in the northern part of the transept, a superb work of Mannerist sculpture from the early 17th century executed by Wolfgang Sparer of Gdańsk. Mannerism also predominates in the Kos family tomb conceived by Willem van den Blocke. The north aisle and ambulatory contain more than a dozen altars of marble in the Baroque style. Baroque forms predominate in the magnificent organ (1763–1788). Compressed air mechanisms direct the movement of the stars, sun and angelic figures during play. The Rococo abbey palace stands next to the cathedral and dates from 1754–56, as do the regular Baroque gardens. A landscape park stretches beyond the gardens.

The cathedral in Pelplin [366] is a more uniform complex. Its Gothic form on the plan of a basilica with a well-defined transept dates from the late 13th century. The desire to keep to a single architectural style is reflected in the late Gothic vaulting which actually comes from 1558. The long, main aisle of superb proportions is closed by a huge main altar (25 m high) made in 1630 and adorned with a painting of *The Coronation of the Madonna* by Hermann Han, a reputed Mannerist painter whose best works were actually conceived in Pelplin. The works of Bartholomew Strobel, court artist to Władysław IV, are also to be found here, as well as those of Andrzej Stech. The Diocesan Museum possesses noteworthy collections housed in the monastery. (P.T.)

The Kaszuby Lake District [367] forms the most easterly part of the Pomeranian Lakeland. The high moraine hills are divided by deep glacial channels filled with finger lakes or marshes, peat bogs left by former lakes or deep river valleys. The River Radunia is one such deep river, carrying water from the

367. Kaszuby Lakeland

368. Kaszuby Lakeland. Raduńskie lake

369. Traditional Kashub costumes

largest glacial channel in the region which contains ten lakes, the largest of which is named after the river: Lake Raduńskie [368]. The lake's area is 1125 hectares and it reaches a depth of 43 m. It is surrounded by farmland, while nearby Lake Ostrzyckie, lying below the Lakeland's highest peak, Wieżyca, is situated among charming beech forests. This region is a popular tourist area for water sports and recreation. The Kaszuby Lakeland in general forms part of a recreational hinterland for the Tri-City agglomeration.

The Carthusian monks, brought over from Prague by the Pomeranian magnate Piotr of Rusocin, built a church and several hermitages on an isthmus between two lakes in 1380–1405. This church and monastery gave rise to a settlement which took the name of Kartuzy. The church with its unusual, coffin-shaped roof dating from 1731–33 can still be admired [365] as well as one remaining hermitage. The existing monastery buildings were pulled down by the Prussians following the partitions and the order's dissolution in 1826. (I.J.K.)

The Kaszuby folk are an autochtonous group of Slavic people living in the Pomerania region. They are offspring of the eastern branch of the old Pomeranians. In 1919, Poland received most of the lands they inhabited, including access to the sea. The rest of their lands were incorporated into Poland in 1945. After almost 150 years of German domination, a young Kaszuby movement developed at the beginning of the 20th century. Its activists attempted to revive the folklore and traditions of Kaszuby, including the characteristic clothes [369].

The Bytów Lakeland adjoins the Kaszuby region. Its main town is Bytów, now a small industrial and tourist centre, existing in the 9th–10th centuries as a Slav stronghold. From the 14th century on it changed hands a number of times between the princes of Gdańsk, Brandenburg and the Teutonic Knights as well as the princes of Western Pomerania. In the years 1390–1405, the Teutonic Knights built a large castle at Bytów [370]. Following the death of the last of the Pomeranian princes in 1637, Bytów was restored to Poland, but not for long, since in 1657 by virtue of the treaty of Wielawa and Bydgoszcz, it was handed over to the Elector of Brandenburg as a fief in return for his aid to Poland during the war against the Swedes. During Prussian rule, Bytów was a major centre of opposition against Germanisation policies, but was not returned to Poland in 1919 by the Treaty of Versailles, in spite of the protests and petitions of its inhabitants. The town was rebuilt after suffering heavy destruction in 1945. The restored castle-residence houses the Western Kaszuby Museum today. (I.J.K.)

370. Bytów. Pomeranian princes' castle

372. Baltic sea

371. Słowiński National Park. Shifting sand dunes

374. Darłowo. Cemetery chapel of St. Gertrude

Poland's longest stretch of seacoast known as the Słowiński Coastal Belt extends westwards from the shores of Kaszuby. It is a narrow strip of low-lying land following the shoreline which has been formed over the past several thousand years – a landscape of beaches, sand-dunes, coastal lakes and marshes. The sea holly is a typical representative of the plant life holding the sand down. The Słowiński Coastal Belt offers excellent conditions for recreation and there are many holiday resorts. Łeba an old fishing settlement attractively situated between the sea and lake Łebskie is the most important seaside town in the eastern part of the Belt. In the vicinity of Łeba, beyond the village of Rąbki, a concrete road leads to the remains of German rocket launch pads set up during the Second World War.

The Słowiński National Park contains the largest complex of shifting sand-dunes in Poland [371] and the sandbanks of Łebsko and Gardno lakes shelter large numbers of a variety of water birds in a strictly protected reservation. Rowokół, a sacred hill to the Pomeranian tribes, together with a number of Slovin villages are also found in the Park. The Slovins were a Pomeranian ethnic group closely related to the Kaszubs who managed to preserve their language, customs and traditional building style for the longest time. Slovin cottages have survived in the village of Kluki. (I.J.K.)

Above the mouth of the River Wieprza, on Darłowo Hill, the Pomeranian stronghold of Darłowo developed in the 11th century. In 1361, the newly-created town joined the Hanseatic League and prospered thereafter into the 15th century. The whole of Western Pomerania came under the rule of Brandenburg by virtue of the Peace of Westphalia in 1648; later Darłowo and the entire province belonged to Prussia. The town was incorporated into Poland in 1945. Some valuable old buildings, largely dating from the period of the Pomeranian Princes, have survived, including the characteristically Pomeranian Gothic cemetery chapel dedicated to St. Gertrude [374], a twelve-sided temple, raised in the 15th century. Today Darłowo is a fishing port [374].

In comparison to the Northern Sea, the yearly fish capacity of the Baltic per one hectare is three times lower. The Baltic sea is a relatively bad habitat for fish but species can be encountered which constitute arctic relics. Several species of fish grow much smaller in the Baltic sea than they do normally. Rockweed is the most popular algae there. Nevertheless, for many Poles and foreign tourists, the Baltic seashore is simply a place to spend the holidays. [372]. (I.J.K.)

373. Darłowo. Fishermen's boats

278

The Drawsko Lakeland occupies the southern, inland area of Koszalin voivodship, containing a large complex of lakes, the most extensive of which are Drawsko and Wielimie. The lakes are linked by rivers, creating charming canoe routes through varied terrain. The principal tourist centres are Szczecinek, Czaplinek and Połczyn Zdrój, the latter being a well-known spa (sorrel, saline and therapeutic mud baths). The village of Stare Drawsko, situated on an isthmus between Drawsko and Żerdno lakes, was the site of a castle built by Casimir the Great in the 14th century, in ruins today [375]. (I.J.K.)

Henryk of Braniewo was among the most celebrated architects of his time capable of breaking with Gothic forms and offering new architectural solutions, including the integration of church interiors through removal of the subdivided presbytery. He also paid considerable attention to exterior decorations, applying delicate and exquisite ceramic bricks. He designed the St.Jacob church in Szczecin, but above all directed the rebuilding of the church of Our Lady in Stargard Szczeciński [376]. A brick hall from the 13th century was adapted into an enormous basilica with an ambulatory and the St.Mary chapel on the axis. The church's interior proportions are particularly impressive [377], partly altered in the 17th century when new vaulting in the Gothic spirit was introduced. The nearby town hall, completed in 1569, has retained its late-Gothic forms. A gable is its most impressive part. (P.T.)

The seaside town and fishing port of Kamień Pomorski is situated on the River Dziwna in the Szczecin Coastland. A port and town was set up here by the Wolin tribe in the 9th – 10th centuries. Later, Kamień became the political capital of Western Pomerania and from 1175, the seat of a bishopric. Municipal status was granted in 1274 and from the early 14th century the town belonged to the Hanseatic League. Kamień was seized in 1630 by the Swedes, who handed it over to Brandenburg in 1679. The growth of a spa and seaside resort began when saline springs were discovered in 1876. The town was largely destroyed in 1945 and occupied by Polish forces. Like all the towns lying on the Szczecin coast, Kamień has many historic monuments. Its medieval urban layout has been preserved, parts of the 13th and 14th century town defences, including the Wolin Gate, a 15th century town hall [382], bishop's palace from the 14th–15th centuries, 18th century canonic manor house and some 18th and 19th century town houses. The cathedral, however, is the town's most highly-prized architectural relic: a late-Romanesque and early-Gothic basilica with a trans-

375. Stare Drawsko. Ruins of Drahim castle

ept (12th – 13th centuries) in which a beautiful 17th century organ [383] has survived. The cathedral treasury houses collections of archeological findings, old religious art and ancient documents. [I.J.K.]

The Bay of Szczecin [378] is what has remained of a sea bay at one time occupying a much greater area. Today it has an area of 968 sq.km, 470 sq.km of which belong to Poland. Its depth does not exceed 7 m. The Bay is linked with the sea by three straits: the Piana (under German administration), Świna and Dziwna. They used to be considerably wider, but have been narrowed by the formation of sand bars. These processes were intensified by the presence of Wolin and Uznam islands dividing the Bay from the Baltic Sea. The Bay is an important shipping route which demands constant regulation. It is also an important fishing area where freshwater and seawater species abound (roach, bream, perch, pike, and eels). [I.J.K.]

Szczecin is the chief town of Western Pomerania and one of Poland's leading ports. It developed on the high left bank of the River Odra not far from the river's estuary. As early as the 9th century, there was a large stronghold on the site, fortified with earth and timber ramparts. In 987, Mieszko I captured Szczecin and incorporated the whole of Pomerania into Poland. Following the death of Bolesław the Brave (1025), the town regained its independence, but around one hundred years later was taken by Bolesław the Wrymouth (1121). In the year 1237, Szczecin was granted municipal status and by 1278 the town had become a member of the Hanseatic League. At the end of the 15th century, Prince Bogusław X transferred the ducal capital of Western Pomerania to Szczecin and built a large castle there. The Thirty Years' War brought great losses and damage to the town and in 1630 it was occupied by the Swedes. As a result of the Northern Wars Szczecin passed into Prussian hands (1713). Sea trade was revived under the Prussians and manufacturing developed. Industry and port facilities were greatly expanded in the later part of the 19th century and a new city centre developed after 1840 on the site of demolished Prussian fortifications. Many Polish migrants arrived in the city from Wielkopolska and Pomerania, although many of their kind emigrated to the new Polish state after 1918. The new political situation created at Versailles led to the port's decline in favour of Hamburg and Gdynia. Many factories closed down during the great economic depression of 1929–1933. During the Second World War;

376. Stargard Szczeciński. Virgin Mary church and town hall

377. Stargard Szczeciński. Interiors of the Virgin Mary church

378. Szczecin Bay

379. Szczecin. Chrobry Embankment

the town, port and industrial infrastructure were severly damaged. The road to reconstruction within the Polish state was long and arduous. The restoration of the city's hinterland greatly aided Szczecin's postwar revival. It is an important transit port for the Czech and Slovak republics, Hungary and the eastern German provinces. Its industries have been expanded together with its cultural and higher educational institutions. The characteristic radiate urban layout of its centre, designed by Haussmann, has remained partly intact. New public buildings and housing estates have been developed. The Chrobry Embankment has retained its early -20th century monumental edifices [379]. Many of Szczecin's more important historic buildings have been restored, including the St. Jacob Cathedral [381], a Gothic hall church, together with the former castle residence of the Dukes of Pomerania [380], restored along Renaissance lines according to original late-16th and early-17th century plans. (I.J.K.)

The National Museum collections in Szczecin, of which the medieval works are the most important, developed in the 19th century thanks to the efforts of individuals who saved many valuable relics from the region's decaying medieval churches. In 1928, the collection was placed in a palace dating from 1727. The medieval section contains numerous wooden and stone objects coming from the 13th -16th centuries; the Gotland late-Romanesque and early-Gothic sculptures are particularly interesting. Renaissance art mostly reflects the Western Pomeranian Dukes' patronage. The arts and crafts collection is also rich. A gallery of 19th and 20th century Polish art was opened in 1948.

The crucifix from Kamień Pomorski cathedral supposedly is the work of Herman Walter of Kołobrzeg (Kolberg). The artist was well acquainted with English and Rhenish sculpture, but produced his own original work inflenced by medieval mysticism. The Madonna statuette from Gardno is associated with the patronage of the Cistercian monastery at Kolbacz. It has been linked by specialists with Gotland sculpture and is an example of late Romanesque art revealing the first signs of Gothic forms. The bronze-cast lock comes from the door of the Kołobrzeg collegiate church and is decorated with a lion's head surrounded by eight medallions entwined with a symbolic grapevine. Symbols of the Evangelists are represented among other motifs on the medallions. The door bolt is assumed to be the work of Johan Apengeter and is considerd a beautiful illustration of Gothic craftsmanship. (P.T.)

380. Szczecin. Southern facade of the Pomeranian princes' castle

381. Szczecin. St. Jacob cathedral

The islands of Wolin and Uznam close the Bay of Szczecin. All of Wolin belongs to Poland since 1945, while Uznam is divided by the border with Germany. In the 7th-9th century both islands were the territory of the Wolinian tribe, whose main settlement was the stronghold of Wolin. The settlements that developed around it were known as a thriving trade centre in the 10th century. Wolin had extensive trade contacts with Scandinavia, northern Germany, Baltic Prussian Sambia and Russian Novgorod. It was attacked and ruined several times in the 11th and 12th centuries by the Danes. Although granted municipal status in 1178 according to German law, the town did not develop. Today Wolin is a small market centre with light industries, but above all a seaside resort. A large part of Wolin Island is covered by luxuriant beech forests [384]. Many rare species of birds are still found here, including the white eagle. A National Park has been set up on the island where certain rarer varieties of trees are also protected. (I.J.K.)

Międzyzdroje lies at the western end of the Wolin National Park; one of the largest and best known spas on the Polish seacoast (saline and mud baths). Formerly an independent urban community at the mouth of the Świna strait separating the two islands, Międzyzdroje was incorporated into Świnoujście in 1973. The centre of Świnoujście is located on the Uznam Island side. The Wolinians had a stronghold on its site in the 9th-10th centuries, but as a town Świnoujście did not really develop until the 18th century, when construction of a port was begun. In the 19th century it expanded as a seaside resort and spa. Today it is a significant deep-water port receiving the largest vessels which cannot gain access to Szczecin because of the Bay's shallowness. It is also the most important deep-sea fishing port in Poland, although Świnoujście does continue to provide many facilities for holiday makers and its spas have been rebuilt or expanded since 1945. There are ferry services to Sweden and Denmark, as well as frequent connections with Szczecin. Long-distance yacht races begin here [386]. (I.J.K.)

382. Kamień Pomorski. Town hall

383. Kamień Pomorski. Organs in the cathedral

384. Wolin National Park

385. Świnoujście. Port

386. Baltic sea. Sunset

Contents:

Introduction   5
Carpathians and Subcarpathians   24
Polish Uplands   78
Sudeten and the Silesian Lowland 128
Wielkopolska Lowland 162
Mazovia and Podlasie Lowland 188
Lakeland and Pomerania 232

Index of contributing photographers:
Araszkiewicz A.: 323; Arczyński S.: 137, 139, 140, 142, 143, 146, 150, 152, 153, 156, 157, 160, 162, 164–166, 172, 173, 183, 189, 205, 215–217, 321; Brym R.: 234; Cała M.: 29, 30, 66, 69, 71; Gadomski S.: 70, 111; Gardzielewska J.: 337; Gąsienica-Byrcyn W.: 19; Górski W.: 357; Grzelec A.: 228, 235, 265; Hermanowicz W.: 64; Jabłońska S.: 4, 6, 20, 25, 28, 36, 37, 38, 52, 53, 56, 59, 63, 68, 75–77, 80, 88, 90, 92, 93, 98, 112–114, 116, 124, 125, 130, 134, 136, 145, 158, 161, 163, 169, 170, 175–177, 179, 180–182, 187, 188, 192–195, 199, 201, 202, 204, 206, 207, 213, 218, 221, 222, 225, 231, 233, 237, 241, 246, 253–255, 262, 264, 268–270, 272, 273, 292, 317, 325–327, 334, 338, 339, 341, 343–346, 353, 361, 362, 368, 370, 374, 376, 377; Jabłoński K.: 39, 42–45, 74, 78, 87, 94, 95, 102, 103, 123, 126, 128, 131, 133, 147, 149, 154, 155, 159, 210, 214, 223, 224, 229, 243–245, 247, 248, 252, 256, 257, 259, 260, 263, 274, 278–280, 283, 293, 294, 322, 328, 329, 331, 333, 335, 340, 347, 349, 350, 351, 354, 355, 360, 364, 366, 371, 380, 381; Kamykowski Z.: 23, 32, 81, 96, 101, 226; Kasperski B.: 46, 100; Kornatowski B.: 89; Korpal J.: 138; Krassowski P.: 54, 55, 58, 84, 104, 105, 109, 151, 211, 212; Krupa C.: 127; Kryński W.: 47, 57, 62, 79, 97, 117, 184, 196, 209, 336, 356, 358; Kupiecki E.: 251, 308; Lesisz A.: 178; Łapiński W.: 18, 49, 288, 289, 296–298, 300, 305, 306, 315; Łuczywek K.: 369; Makarewicz J.: 373, 378; Michta S.: 85; Morek J.: 22, 33; Ochnio W.: 291; Okoński W.: 249, 261, 386; Olszewski T.: 7; Pierściński P.: cover, 60, 65, 106–108, 110, 118, 121, 135; Plebankiewicz K.: 132, 141, 144, 148, 186, 198, 230, 277; Podziewski J.: 303; Pokropek M.: 290; Raczkowski M.: 31, 41, 50, 220, 227; Sadowski S.: 35, 365; Sawicki L.K.: 304; Siemaszko Z.: 250, 271, 276; Siudecki J.: 236; Sobieszczuk I.: 119; Sowiński Z.: 73; Stasiak W.: 34, 40, 72, 83, 122, 129, 167, 171, 174, 191, 197, 200, 208, 219, 232, 240, 258, 275, 281, 324, 330, 332, 348; Stelmach A.: 67; Strojny W.: 185; Sumiński T.: insert I, 1, 5, 21, 24, 26, 27, 48, 51, 82, 86, 120, 238, 239, 242, 282, 285–287, 299, 301, 302, 307, 310–314, 316, 318–320, 363, 367, 372; Surowiec L.: 309; Szymański A.: 375; Uklejewski J.: 352, 359; Unierzyski J.: 203; Witusz A.: 385; Wołkow W.: 295; Wróblewski L.: 61, 266; Ziemak R.: insert II, 2, 3, 168, 267, 284, 379, 382–384; Zwolińska Z.: 8–17; Żak J.: 91, 99; Arkady Publishing House archives: 115, 342.

Introduction:
Wojciech Giełżyński

Translated by
„Multilanguage" & Peter Martin

Copy – editing:
Arkady Publishing House editorial office

Photograph selection:
Andrzej Łotysz

Design:
Jerzy Kępkiewicz

Typographic design:
Wiesław Pyszka

CIP - Biblioteka Narodowa
Poland : Carpathians and Subcarpathians,
Polish Uplands, Sudeten and the Silesian Lowland,
Wielkopolska Lowland, Mazovia and Polesie Lowland,
Lakeland and Pomerania / Wojciech Giełżyński,
Irena and Jerzy Kostrowicki, [transl. from pol. Peter
Martin]. - [4 ed.]. - Warszawa : „Arkady" , 1999

Arkady - Publishing House Ltd., 00-344 Warsaw,
28 Dobra Street. 4th edition, 1999. Symbol 21935/R
Typesetting and layout - Comptext, Warsaw
Printed by Fournier Artes Graficas S.A.,
Vitoria - Spain